WILD ABOUT
DINOSAURS

WILD ABOUT
DINOSAURS

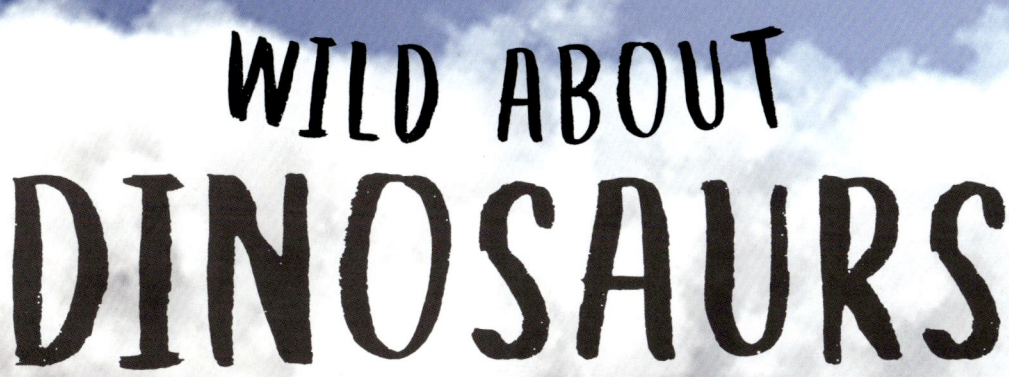

WRITTEN BY
RUPERT MATTHEWS, STEVE PARKER

Little Hippo Books

First published in 2017 by Miles Kelly Publishing Ltd
Harding's Barn, Bardfield End Green, Thaxted, Essex, CM6 3PX, UK

Copyright © Miles Kelly Publishing Ltd 2017

2 4 6 8 10 9 7 5 3 1

Publishing Director Belinda Gallagher
Creative Director Jo Cowan
Editorial Director Rosie Neave
Senior Editor Fran Bromage
Editorial Assistant Meghan Oosterhuis
Cover Designer Joe Jones
Designers Rob Hale, Joe Jones, Andrea Slane
Image Manager Liberty Newton
Indexer Jane Parker
Production Elizabeth Collins
Reprographics Stephan Davis
Assets Venita Kidwai

Consultants Camilla de la Bedoyere, Steve Parker

All rights reserved. No part of this publication may be reproduced, stored in a retrieval system, or transmitted by any means, electronic, mechanical, photocopying, recording, or otherwise, without the prior permission of the copyright holder.

ISBN 978-1-960009-28-9

Printed in China

Made with paper from a sustainable forest

littlehippobooks.com

Contents

PREHISTORIC LIFE — 6
- Life begins — 8
- Animals swarm the seas — 10
- Very fishy — 12
- Animals invade the land — 14
- Life after death — 16
- Wars around the world — 18
- Reptiles take over — 20
- Living with the dinosaurs — 22
- In and over the sea — 24
- After the dinosaurs — 26
- As the world cooled down — 28
- Prehistoric prowlers — 30
- Amazing ancient elephants — 32
- Animals with hooves — 34
- Cats, dogs, and bears — 36
- Prehistoric giants — 38
- Our prehistoric relations — 40

DINOSAURS — 42
- When were dinosaurs alive? — 44
- Before the dinosaurs — 46
- Dinosaurs arrive — 48
- First of the giants — 50
- What teeth tell us — 52
- Supersize dinosaurs — 54
- Killer claws — 56
- Deadly meat-eaters — 58
- Look! Listen! Sniff! — 60
- Living with dinosaurs — 62
- How fast? — 64
- Built like tanks — 66
- Nests and eggs — 68
- Dinosaur babies — 70
- The end for the dinosaurs — 72
- What happened next? — 74

T-REX — 76
- Terror of its age — 78
- A giant predator — 80
- Profile of *T-Rex* — 82
- Was *T-Rex* clever? — 84
- What big teeth — 86
- Tiny arms, big legs — 88
- What did *T-Rex* eat? — 90
- Hunter or scavenger? — 92
- Growing up — 94
- Where in the world? — 96
- Tyrannosaur group — 98
- Close cousins — 100
- Discovering *T-Rex* — 102
- Rebuilding *T-Rex* — 104
- The story of Sue — 106
- Stan, Jane, and the rest — 108
- Bigger than the "king" — 110
- *T-Rex* superstar — 112
- What next for *T-Rex*? — 114

FOSSILS — 116
- What are fossils? — 118
- Fossils get scientific — 120
- How fossils form — 122
- Mold and cast fossils — 124
- Special preservation — 126
- Fossils and time — 128
- Working out dates — 130
- How many years ago? — 132
- Fossil-hunting takes off — 134
- Dinosaurs today — 136
- Famous hot spots — 138
- Looking for fossils — 140
- At the dig — 142
- Cleaning up fossils — 144
- On display — 146
- Fossils come alive! — 148
- Trading, stealing, faking — 150
- Famous fossils — 152
- Looking to the future — 154

INDEX — 156
ACKNOWLEDGMENTS — 160

PREHISTORIC LIFE

1 The Earth was once covered by huge sheets of ice. This happened several times during Earth's history and we call these frozen times ice ages. However, the ice ages are a tiny part of prehistory. Before then, the world was warm and lakes and seas covered the land. Even earlier than this, there was little rain for thousands of years, and the land was covered in deserts. Over millions of years weather and conditions changed. Living things changed too, in order to survive. This change is called "evolution."

Woolly rhinoceros

Cave lion

▼ A scene from the last ice age, about 10,000 years ago. Animals grew thick fur coats to protect themselves from the cold. Many animals, such as woolly mammoths, survived on plants such as mosses. Others, such as cave lions, were fierce hunters, needing meat to survive.

Aurochs

Wooly mammoth

Megaloceros

Life begins

▼ Fossils of *Anomalocaris* have been found in Canada. It had a circular mouth and finlike body parts. Its body was covered by a shell.

2 **Life began a very, very long time ago.** We know this from the remains of prehistoric life forms that died and were buried. Over millions of years, their remains turned into shapes in rocks, called fossils. The first fossils are over 3 billion years old. They are tiny "blobs" called bacteria—living things that still survive today.

3 **The first plants were seaweeds, which appeared about 1 billion years ago.** Unlike bacteria and blue-green algae, which each had just one living cell, these plants had thousands of cells. Some seaweeds were many feet long. They were called algae—the same name that scientists use today.

4 **By about 800 million years ago, some plants were starting to grow on land.** They were mixed with other living things called molds, or fungi. Together, the algae (plants) and fungi formed flat green-and-yellow crusts that crept over rocks and soaked up rain. They were called lichens. These still grow on rocks and trees today.

PREHISTORIC LIFE

5 **The first animals lived in the sea—and they were as soft as gelatin!** Over 600 million years ago, some of the first animals were jellyfish, floating in the water. On the seabed lived groups of soft, feathery-looking creatures called *Charnia*. This animal was an early type of coral. Animals need to take in food by eating other living things. *Charnia* caught tiny plants in its "feathers."

◀ *Charnia* looked like a prehistoric plant, but it was actually an animal!

6 **One of the first hunting animals was *Anomalocaris*.** It lived 520 million years ago, swimming through the sea in search of prey. It caught smaller creatures in its pincers, then pushed them into its mouth. *Anomalocaris* was a cousin of crabs and insects. It was one of the biggest hunting animals of its time, even though it was only 2 feet long.

7 **By 400 million years ago, plants on land were growing taller.** They had stiff stems that held them upright and carried water to their topmost parts. An early upright plant was *Cooksonia*. It was the tallest living thing on land, at just 2 inches tall—hardly the size of your thumb!

▲ The *Cooksonia* plant had forked stems that carried water. The earliest examples have been found in Ireland.

Animals swarm the seas

8 **Some of the first common animals were worms.** However, they were not earthworms in soil. At the time there was no soil and the land was bare. These worms lived in the sea. They burrowed in mud for plants and animals to eat.

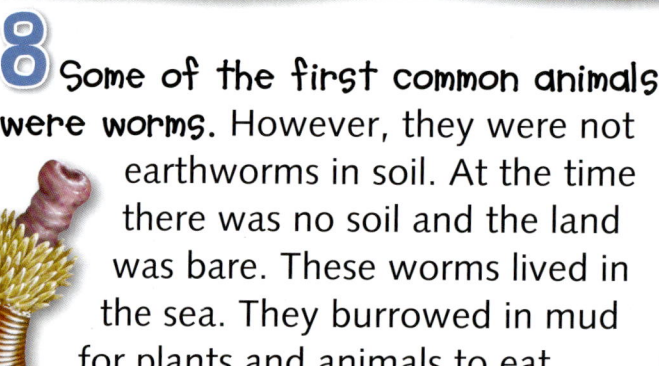

▼ Trilobites moved quickly across the seabed. Some could roll up into a ball like pill bugs do today. This was a means of protection.

◄ *Ottoia* was a sea worm that fed by filtering tiny food particles from the sea.

9 **The next animals to become common were trilobites.** They first lived about 550 million years ago in the sea. Trilobites crawled along the seabed eating tiny bits of food they found. Their name means "three lobes" (parts). A trilobite had two grooves along its back, from head to tail, so its body had three main parts—left, middle, and center.

10 **Trilobites were some of the first animals with legs that bent at the joints.** Animals with jointed legs are called arthropods. They have been the most common creatures for millions of years, including trilobites long ago, and later on, crabs, spiders, and insects. Like other arthropods, trilobites had a tough, outer shell for protection.

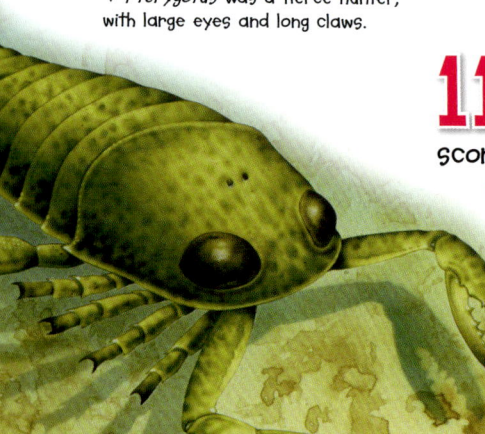

▼ *Pterygotus* was a fierce hunter, with large eyes and long claws.

11 **Some of the first hunters were sea scorpions—some were as big as lions!** *Pterygotus* was 6.5 feet long. It swished its tail to chase prey through water, which it tore apart with its huge claws. Sea scorpions lived 500–250 million years ago. Unlike modern scorpions, they had no sting in their tails.

PREHISTORIC LIFE

12 For millions of years the seabed was covered with the curly shells of ammonites. Some of these shells were as small as your fingernail, others were bigger than dinner plates. Ammonites were successful creatures and thousands of kinds survived for millions of years. Each ammonite had big eyes to see prey and long tentacles (arms) to catch it with. Ammonites died out at the same time as the dinosaurs, around 65 million years ago.

▲ This rock contains an ammonite fossil. The shell would have protected the soft-bodied creature inside.

◄ *Pikaia* looked a little bit like an eel with fins.

13 Among the worms, trilobites, and ammonites was a small creature that had a very special body part—the beginnings of a backbone. It was called *Pikaia* and lived about 530 million years ago. Gradually, more animals with backbones, called vertebrates, evolved from it. Today, vertebrates rule much of the world—they are fish, reptiles, birds, and mammals.

QUIZ

1. Did sea scorpions have stings in their tails?
2. What does the name "trilobite" mean?
3. What kind of animal was *Ottoia*?
4. When did ammonites die out?
5. What was special about *Pikaia*?

Answers:
1. No 2. Three lobes, or parts 3. A worm 4. 65 million years ago 5. It had an early type of backbone

Very fishy

14 **The first fish could not bite—they were suckers!** About 500 million years ago, new animals appeared in the sea—the first fish. They had no jaws or teeth and probably sucked in worms and small pieces of food from the mud.

▲ *Hemicyclaspis* was an early jawless fish. It had eyes on top of its head and probably lived on the seabed. This way it could keep a look out for predators above.

15 **Some early fish wore suits of armor!** They had hard, curved plates of bone all over their bodies for protection. These fish were called placoderms and most were fierce hunters. Some had huge jaws with sharp sheets of bone for slicing up prey.

16 **Spiny sharks had spines, but they were not really sharks.** These fish were similar in shape to today's sharks, but they lived in rivers and lakes, not the sea, about 430 million years ago. *Climatius* was a spiny shark that looked fierce, but it was only as big as your finger!

◀ The fins on the back of *Climatius* were supported by needle-sharp spines. These helped to protect it from attacks by squid or other fish.

PREHISTORIC LIFE

17 **The first really big hunting fish was bigger than today's great white shark!** *Dunkleosteus* grew to around 30 feet in length and swam in the oceans 360 million years ago. It sliced up prey, such as other fish, using its massive teeth made of narrow blades of bone, each one as big as this book.

18 **Some early fish started to "walk" out of water.** Types of fish called lobefins appeared 390 million years ago. Their side fins each had a "stump" at the base made of muscle. If the water in their pool dried up, lobefins could use their fins like stubby legs to waddle over land to another pool. *Eusthenopteron* was a lobefin fish about 3 feet long. Over millions of years, some lobefins evolved into four-legged animals called tetrapods.

VERY FISHY!

You will need:
waxed cardboard (like the kind used to make milk cartons)   crayons   scissors   piece of soap

Place the piece of waxed cardboard face down, fold it up at the edges, and draw a fish on it. With help from an adult, cut a small notch in the rear of the cardboard and wedge the piece of soap in it. Put the "fish" in a bath of cold water and watch it swim away.

▼ *Eusthenopteron* could clamber about on dry land when moving from one stretch of water to another.

Animals invade the land

19 **The first land animals lived about 450 million years ago.** These early creatures, which came from the sea, were arthropods—creatures with hard outer body casings and jointed legs. They included prehistoric insects, spiders, and millipedes. *Arthropleura* was a millipede—it was 6.5 feet in length!

▶ *Arthropleura* was as long as a human and was the largest-ever land arthropod.

20 **Some amphibians were fierce hunters.** *Gerrothorax* was about 3 feet long and spent most of its time at the bottom of ponds or streams. Its eyes pointed upward, to see fish swimming past, just above. *Gerrothorax* would then jump up to grab the fish in its wide jaws.

21 **The first four-legged animal had eight toes on each front foot!** *Acanthostega* used its toes to grip water plants as it swam. It lived about 380 million years ago and was 3 feet long. Creatures like it soon began to walk on land, too. They were called tetrapods, which means "four legs." They were a big advance in evolution—the first land animals with backbones.

◀ *Acanthostega* probably spent most of its time in water. It had gills for breathing underwater as well as lungs for breathing air.

PREHISTORIC LIFE

22 Soon four-legged animals called amphibians were racing across the land. Amphibians were the first backboned animals to move fast out of the water. *Aphaneramma* had long legs and could run quickly. However, prehistoric amphibians, like those of today such as frogs and newts, had to return to the water to lay their eggs.

23 Fins became legs for walking on land, and tails changed, too. As the fins of lobefin fish evolved into legs, their tails became longer and more muscular. *Ichthyostega* had a long tail with a fin along its upper side. This tail design was good for swimming in water, and also helpful when wriggling across a swamp.

24 Some amphibians grew as big as crocodiles! *Eogyrinus* was around 16 feet long and had strong jaws and teeth, like a crocodile. However, it lived about 300 million years ago, long before any crocodiles appeared. Although *Eogyrinus* could walk on dry land, it spent most of its time in streams and swamps.

◀ *Ichthyostega* had short legs, so it could probably only move slowly on land.

Life after death

25 **There were times in prehistory when almost everything died out.** These times are called mass extinctions. Just a few types of plants and animals survive, which can then change, or evolve, into new kinds. A mass extinction about 290 million years ago allowed a fairly new group of animals to spread fast—the reptiles.

26 **Reptiles' skin and eggs helped them to survive.** Unlike an amphibian's, a reptile's scaly skin was waterproof. Also, the gelatin-like eggs of amphibians had to be laid in water, while a reptile's eggs had tough shells for surviving on land. Around 280 million years ago, reptiles such as 5-foot-long *Varanosaurus* were spreading to dry areas where amphibians could not survive.

▲ *Varanosaurus* lived in what is now Texas, and may have hunted fish in swamps.

EDIBLE REPTILES!

You will need:
3.5 oz powdered milk   3.5 oz smooth peanut butter   2 tablespoons honey   currants   food coloring   gloves

Mix the dried milk, peanut butter, and honey in a bowl. Mold this paste into reptile shapes. Decorate with currants for eyes and, using gloves, add food coloring for bright skin patterns. Then cause a mass extinction—eat them!

PREHISTORIC LIFE

▶ *Hylonomus* lived in forests in what is now Canada. It hunted insects, spiders, and millipedes.

27 **The first reptile looked like a lizard.** However *Hylonomus* belonged to a different reptile group to lizards. It lived like a lizard, chasing prey on the ground and in trees. It lived 345 million years ago.

28 **Some reptiles started to avoid bad weather by sleeping underground.** *Diictodon* lived about 260 million years ago and used its large teeth to chop up tough plant food. It may have dug holes to shelter from the heat, cold, and rain.

▼ *Diictodon* had strong legs and sharp claws for burrowing.

Wars around the world

▼ The nostrils and eyes of *Mastodonsaurus* were on top of its head so that it could breathe and look around while hiding underwater.

29 Some amphibians fought back against the reptiles. *Mastodonsaurus* was a big, strong amphibian, 6.5 feet long, with sharp teeth. It hunted fish, other amphibians, and small reptiles. It lived at a time when reptiles were spreading even faster, about 250–203 million years ago. But most other big amphibians did not survive the reptiles.

30 Other amphibians managed to survive the reptile takeover, too. They were mainly small and hid in water or swamps. One was *Branchiosaurus*, which was about 5 inches long and hunted small fish in ponds.

PREHISTORIC LIFE

31 *Lystrosaurus may have had tusks sticking out of its nose!* Two front teeth may have poked through holes at the end of its snout.

▲ *Lystrosaurus* lived in Antarctica when it was a land of lush, tropical plant life. Today it is a frozen continent, covered by thick ice.

32 *Reptiles showed how the world's lands moved about.* Lystrosaurus lived about 200 million years ago and its fossils come from Europe, Asia, Africa, and Antarctica. This reptile could not swim, so all of these landmasses, or continents, must have been joined together at one time. Over millions of years, they drifted apart to form today's positions.

33 *Some plant-eating reptiles had very sharp teeth.* Moschops was as big as a rhino and lived in southern Africa about 270 million years ago. Its teeth were long and straight, and ended with a sharp edge like a chisel. *Moschops* could easily bite tough leaves and twigs off bushes.

▶ As well as sharp teeth, *Moschops* had very strong skull bones, so it may have head-butted rivals in fights.

Reptiles take over

34 **Reptiles don't like to be too hot, or too cold.** Otherwise they may overheat, or be too cold to move. Most reptiles bask in sunshine to get warm, then stay in the shade. *Dimetrodon* was a fierce reptile. It had a large "sail" of skin on its back to soak up heat from the sun.

▲ The name *Dimetrodon* means "two-types-of-teeth." It was given this name as it had stabbing teeth and slicing teeth. It measured 10 feet in length.

QUIZ

1. How did *Dimetrodon* get warm?
2. Which types of reptile evolved into mammals?
3. How did some early reptiles swim?
4. Did the first crocodiles like water?

Answers:
1. By basking in the sun 2. Therapsids 3. By swishing their tails from side to side 4. No, they hated it!

35 **The first crocodiles hated water!** An early type of crocodile, *Protosuchus*, stayed on land. It lived in North America about 190 million years ago. It was 3 feet long and could run across dry land when hunting, using its long legs.

▶ *Protosuchus* had very powerful jaw muscles to snap its teeth shut on prey.

▶ *Chasmatosaurus* had teeth on the roof of its mouth as well as in its jaws.

36 **Some reptiles moved by using their tails.** Many types of early reptiles had long, strong tails. They probably lived in water and swished their tails to push themselves along. *Chasmatosaurus* was 6.5 feet long and probably hunted for fish. It looked like a crocodile but was more closely related to the dinosaurs.

37 **Some reptiles began to look very much like mammals.** *Cynognathus* was as big as a large dog, and instead of scaly skin it was covered in fur. It belonged to a group of reptiles called therapsids. Around 220 million years ago, some types of small therapsids were evolving into the first mammals.

◀ The jaws of *Cynognathus* were so powerful they could bite through bone. Its name means "dog jaw."

Living with the dinosaurs

38 Some reptiles were as big and fierce as dinosaurs, but they lived in the sea. One of these was *Mosasaurus*. It grew to around 30 feet long and may have weighed over 10 tons—far bigger than today's great white shark.

39 Fossils of *Mosasaurus* were found in the same place over 200 years apart! The first was found in a quarry in the Netherlands in 1780. The second was found in the same place in 1998.

40 One sea reptile had teeth the size of saucers! The huge, round, flat teeth of *Placodus* were more than 4 inches across. It used them to crush shellfish and sea urchins. *Placodus* was 6.5 feet long and lived at the same time as the first dinosaurs, about 230 million years ago.

▼ *Mosasaurus* was a huge sea reptile. It had razor-sharp teeth and could swim with speed to catch its prey.

PREHISTORIC LIFE

▼ *Archaeopteryx* had a long bony tail, unlike modern birds, which have no bones in their tails.

41 **Fossils of the first bird were mistaken for a dinosaur.** *Archaeopteryx* lived in Europe about 155 million years ago. Some of its fossils look very similar to the fossils of small dinosaurs. So *Archaeopteryx* was thought to be a dinosaur, until scientists saw the faint shape of its feathers and realized it was a bird.

42 **Soon there were many kinds of birds flying above the dinosaurs.** *Confuciusornis* was about 2 feet long and lived in what is now China, 120 million years ago. It had a backward-pointing big toe on each foot, which suggests it climbed through the trees. It is also the earliest known bird to have a true beak.

▲ Fossils of *Confuciusornis* have been found in China. It is named after the famous Chinese wise man, Confucius.

43 **Mammals lived at the same time as dinosaurs.** These animals have warm blood, and fur or hair, unlike a reptile's scaly skin. *Megazostrodon* was the earliest mammal known to scientists. It lived in southern Africa about 215 million years ago—only 15 million years or so after the dinosaurs began life on Earth. It was just 5 inches long, and probably hunted insects.

▼ *Megazostrodon* probably came out at night to hunt for its insect prey. It looked a little like a modern-day shrew.

In and over the sea

44 **One prehistoric reptile had the bendiest neck ever!** The sea reptile *Elasmosaurus* had a neck over 16 feet long—the same as three people lying head to toe. Its neck was so bendy that *Elasmosaurus* could twist it around in a circle as it looked for fish and other creatures to eat.

45 **The first big flying animals were not birds, but pterosaurs.** They lived at the same time as the dinosaurs, and died out at the same time too, about 65 million years ago. *Pteranodon* was one of the later pterosaurs and lived about 70 million years ago. It swooped over the sea to scoop up fish.

▼ *Pteranodon* scoops up prey while long-necked *Elasmosaurus* snaps its jaws in search of food.

Pteranodon

PREHISTORIC LIFE

46 The largest flying animal of all time was as big as a plane! With wings measuring up to 45 feet from tip to tip, the pterosaur *Quetzalcoatlus* was twice as big as any flying bird. It may have lived like a vulture, soaring high in the sky, and then landing to peck at a dead body of a dinosaur.

47 Some fossils of sea creatures are found thousands of miles from the sea. Around 100 to 70 million years ago, much of what is now North America was flooded. The shallow waters teemed with all kinds of fish, reptiles, and other creatures. Today their fossils are found on dry land.

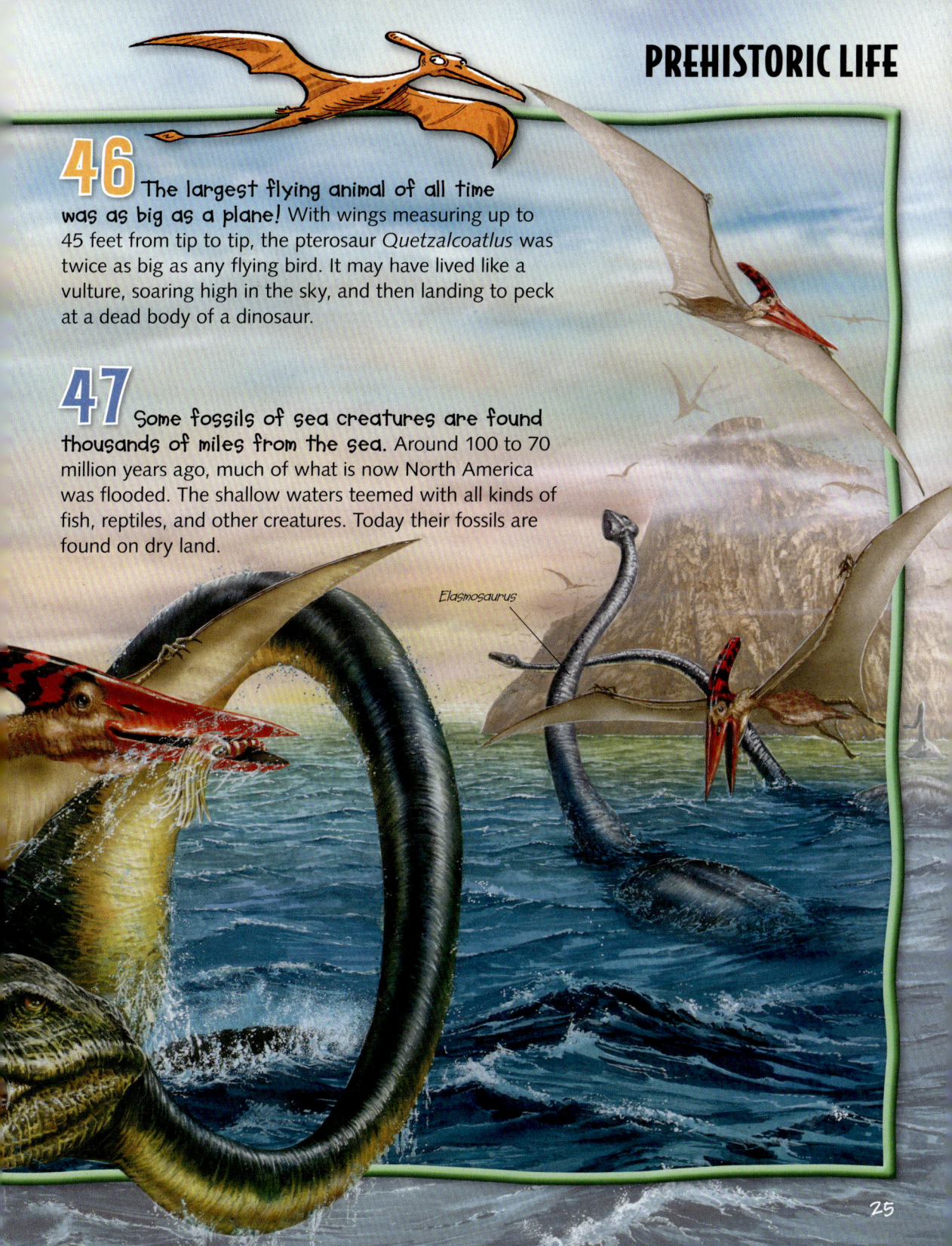

Elasmosaurus

After the dinosaurs

48 **A disaster about 66 million years ago killed off the dinosaurs and many other creatures.** The main new group of animals was the mammals. Most were small, like rats and mice. *Leptictidium* lived 50–40 million years ago. It may be related to moles and shrews.

▲ *Leptictidium* probably hopped like a kangaroo!

50 **Often the name of a prehistoric animal can be misleading, like *Palaeotherium*, which simply means "ancient animal."** However this name was given over 200 years ago, in 1804, because scientists of the time did not know as much as modern scientists. Later studies show that *Palaeotherium* was one of the first animals in the group of hoofed mammals that includes horses.

◀ *Pakicetus* is the earliest known whale.

49 **Whales began life on dry land and gradually returned to the sea.** *Pakicetus* lived about 50 million years ago and was nearly 7 feet long. It probably spent a lot of time on land as well as in water.

PREHISTORIC LIFE

▼ A mother *Uintatherium* and her baby. This strange-looking creature was the largest land animal of its time. Its head was covered in horns and it had small tusks.

51 Around 40 million years ago, the largest animal walking the Earth was *Uintatherium*. This plant-eater was around 10 feet long and nearly 7 feet tall at the shoulder—about the same size as a cow. Its fossils were found near the Uinta River in Colorado. *Uintatherium* is thought to be a cousin of horses and elephants.

52 An animal's looks can be misleading. *Patriofelis* means "father of the cats." It lived about 45 million years ago and was named because scientists thought it was an early cat. Later they realized that it merely looked like a cat. It was really a member of an extinct group of hunting animals called creodonts.

QUIZ

1. What does the name *Patriofelis* mean?
2. How long was *Pakicetus*?
3. In what year were *Palaeotherium* fossils found?
4. How tall was *Uintatherium*?
5. When did dinosaurs die out and mammals start to take over?

Answers:
1. "Father of the cats" 2. About 7 feet 3. 1804 4. Almost 7 feet tall at the shoulder 5. 65 million years ago

As the world cooled down

53 Before the world started to cool 30 million years ago, palm trees grew almost everywhere—but they became rare. These trees had thrived in warm, wet conditions. But as Earth cooled, other plants took over, such as magnolias, pines, oaks, and birch. These changes meant that animals changed too.

▼ *Brontotherium* was somewhere in size between a rhino and an elephant. Males used the Y-shaped horn on their snouts in fighting competitions.

54 *Pyrotherium* means "fire beast," but not because this plant-eater could walk through fire. Its fossils were found in layers of ash from an ancient volcano in Argentina, South America. The volcano probably erupted, and its fumes and ash suffocated and burned all the animals nearby. *Pyrotherium* was about as big as a cow and looked like a combination of a pig and a short-tusked elephant.

55 Many prehistoric animals have exciting names— *Brontotherium* means "thunder beast." Where the fossils of *Brontotherium* were found in North America, local people thought they were bones of the gods. They thought that these gods rode chariots across the sky and started thunderstorms, which led to the animal's name.

PREHISTORIC LIFE

56 *Andrewsarchus* was a real big-head! At 3 feet long, it had the biggest head of any hunting mammal on land, and its strong jaws were filled with sharp, pointed teeth. Its whole body was bigger than a tiger of today. *Andrewsarchus* probably lived like a hyena, crunching up bones and gristle from dead animals. Yet it belonged to a mammal group that was mostly plant-eaters. It lived 30 million years ago in what is now the deserts of Mongolia, Asia.

▲ *Andrewsarchus* was the biggest meat-eating land mammal ever to have lived.

I DON'T BELIEVE IT!
Even if global warming carries on, the world will not be as hot as it was 35 million years ago.

▲ The horns on *Arsinoitherium's* head were hollow and may have been used to make mating calls.

57 Some animals had horns as tall as people! *Arsinoitherium's* two massive horns looked like powerful weapons—but they were light, fragile, and made of very thin bone. This plant-eater lived in northern Africa about 35 million years ago. It was almost as big as an elephant and may have been an ancient cousin of the elephant group.

Prehistoric prowlers

58 Some animals probably ate just about anything. Entelodonts were piglike animals that lived about 25 million years ago. *Dinohyus* was one of the largest entelodonts. Its teeth were sharp and strong, and it had powerful jaw muscles. It ate almost anything from leaves, roots, and seeds, to small animals.

59 Some predators (hunting animals) walked on tiptoe but others were flat-footed. Most mammal predators, such as cats and dogs, walk on the ends of their toes. This helps them to run faster. *Daphoenodon* walked on flat feet, like a bear. It is often called a "bear-dog" as it looked like a dog but walked like a bear.

▼ *Dinohyus* lived in North America and grew to be about 10 feet long. Its powerful neck muscles and large canine teeth suggest it could have broken bones and eaten flesh.

PREHISTORIC LIFE

60 Fossils can show if predators hunted by day or at night. *Plesictis* was a weasel-like hunter, and its fossils show it had large sockets (spaces) for its eyes. This means that it probably hunted at night. It also had sharp claws and a long tail, so it may have scampered through trees hunting birds and insects, gripping tightly with its claws and balancing with its tail.

61 Some predators have changed little over millions of years. *Potamotherium* was an early otter and lived in Europe, 23 million years ago. It looked almost like the otters of today. Its shape was so well-suited to hunting fish in streams that it has hardly changed.

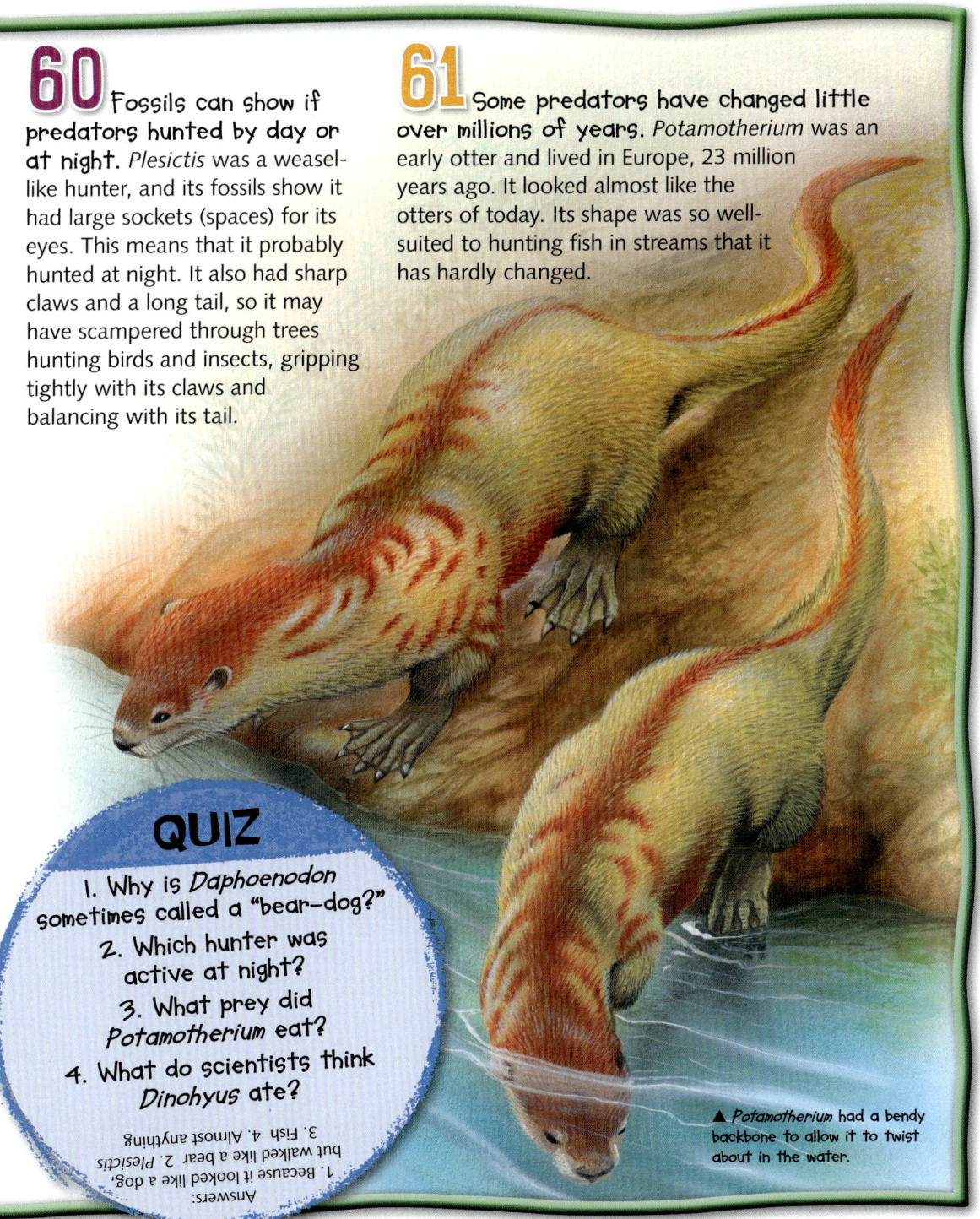

▲ *Potamotherium* had a bendy backbone to allow it to twist about in the water.

QUIZ

1. Why is *Daphoenodon* sometimes called a "bear-dog?"
2. Which hunter was active at night?
3. What prey did *Potamotherium* eat?
4. What do scientists think *Dinohyus* ate?

Answers:
1. Because it looked like a dog, but walked like a bear 2. *Plesictis* 3. Fish 4. Almost anything

Amazing ancient elephants

62 **The first elephant had tiny tusks and almost no trunk.** *Moeritherium* lived in northern Africa about 36 million years ago. It stood just 2 feet tall and weighed around 40 pounds—about the size of a pet dog.

▶ Woolly mammoths had coats of shaggy hair. This hair kept their warm inner fur dry and waterproof in the freezing conditions of the ice age.

I DON'T BELIEVE IT!
The tusks of *Anancus* were more than 13 feet long—almost as long as the animal itself.

63 **Some elephants were very hairy.** The woolly mammoth was covered in thick, long, dense hair to keep out the cold of the ice age. It was larger than a modern elephant and was probably hunted by early people. The last woolly mammoths may have died out less than 10,000 years ago.

64 **One elephant had tusks like shovels.** *Platybelodon* lived about nine million years ago in Europe, Asia, and Africa. Its lower tusks were shaped like broad, flat shovels. Perhaps it used them to scoop up water plants to eat.

PREHISTORIC LIFE

66 Some elephants had four tusks. *Tetralophodon* lived about eight million years ago and stood 10 feet tall. Its fossils have been found in Europe, Asia, Africa, and America, so it was a very widespread and successful animal.

67 The biggest elephant was the Columbian mammoth. It was 13 feet tall and may have weighed over 11 tons—twice as much as most elephants today. It lived on the grasslands of southern North America.

▼ The Columbian mammoth had tusks that twisted into curved, spiral shapes.

65 Elephants were more varied and common long ago, than they are today. *Anancus* roamed Europe and Asia two million years ago. Like modern elephants, it used its trunk to pull leaves from branches and its tusks to dig up roots. However most kinds of prehistoric elephants died out. Only two kinds survive today, in Africa and Asia.

Animals with hooves

68 The first horse was hardly larger than a pet cat. *Hyracotherium* lived in Europe, Asia, and North America about 50 million years ago. It was only 8 inches tall and lived in woods and forests.

▲ *Hyracotherium* is sometimes called *Eohippus*, which means "dawn horse." It had a short neck, slender legs, and a long tail.

69 Early horses did not eat grass—because there wasn't any. Grasses and open plains did not appear on Earth until 25 million years ago. Then early horses moved onto them, started to eat grass, and gradually became bigger.

70 Over millions of years, horses gradually lost their toes! The very first horses had five toes per foot, each ending in a small nail-like hoof. *Hyracotherium* had four toes on each front foot and three on each back foot. Later, *Mesohippus*, which was as big as a labrador dog, had three toes on each foot. Today's horses have just one toe on each foot, which ends in a large hoof.

PREHISTORIC LIFE

71 **Some prehistoric camels had horns.** *Synthetoceras* had a pair of horns at the top of its head, and also a peculiar Y-shaped horn growing from its nose. It probably used these horns to fight enemies and also to show off to others of its kind at breeding time.

▶ The amazing nose horn of *Synthetoceras* was present only on male animals.

▼ *Megaloceros* may have stored food for the winter in the form of fat in a hump on its shoulder.

72 **Thousands of years ago, horses died out in the Americas.** Spanish travelers reintroduced horses to this area about 500 years ago.

73 **Some prehistoric deer had antlers as big as a person!** *Megaloceros* means "big deer" and it was as big as today's biggest deer, the moose. But its antlers were even bigger, measuring almost 13 feet from tip to tip. *Megaloceros* may have survived in some parts of Europe until as little as 3,000 years ago.

Cats, dogs, and bears

74 The sabertooth "tiger" *Smilodon* had two huge sharp teeth like sabers (swords)—but it was not really a tiger. It belonged to a different group of cats to real tigers. *Smilodon*'s teeth were long and sharp but not very strong. It probably used them like knives to stab and slash at its prey, which then bled to death. *Smilodon* then ate it without a struggle.

▶ *Smilodon* had enormously powerful shoulders, so it may have sprung on its prey and held it down.

75 The earliest cats were similar to those of today. *Dinictis* lived about 30 million years ago and was strong and stealthy, like the modern-day cougar (mountain lion). It probably hunted like modern cats too, by creeping up close to a victim, then leaping on it to bite its throat or neck.

76 The first dog, *Hesperocyon*, had a long body and short legs, more like a stoat or mongoose. It was about 3 feet long and lived about 30 million years ago. Only later dogs had long legs and were able to run fast after their prey.

◀ *Hesperocyon* may have hunted in packs. This would have allowed it to hunt animals much larger than itself.

PREHISTORIC LIFE

77 The sabertooth "cat" *Thylacosmilus* was not even a real cat! It had a cat-shaped head, body, legs, and tail. Yet it was a marsupial—a cousin of kangaroos and koalas. It lived in South America four million years ago.

78 Sea lions did not develop from lions—but from dogs. *Allodesmus* was an early type of sea lion and lived about 13 million years ago. It had strong flippers for fast swimming. Its fossil bones show that it came originally from the dog group.

◀ Early humans had to face many natural dangers, such as cave bears.

79 Early people hunted cave bears, and cave bears hunted early people! The huge cave bear of the Ice Age was as big as today's grizzly bear. Humans called Neanderthals hunted them and used their bones and teeth as ornaments. The bears hunted people too, and left their bones in caves.

Prehistoric giants

80 The largest flying bird ever was as big as a small plane! *Argentavis* was twice the size of any flying bird today. Its wings measured 23 feet from tip to tip. It was a huge vulture that fed on the dead bodies of other creatures, tearing off their flesh with its powerful hooked beak.

▼ *Argentavis* lived about seven million years ago in South America.

81 Some birds were even bigger than *Argentavis*, but they could not fly—and they were deadly hunters. In South America about one million years ago, *Titanis* grew to 10 feet tall. It raced after its prey, which it tore apart with its huge, hooked beak.

82 A type of prehistoric kangaroo, *Procoptodon*, was twice as big as those of today. Yet it could bound along as fast as a racehorse. Like kangaroos of today, it was a marsupial, carrying its baby in a pouch. It lived in Australia.

▶ In South America, *Titanis* was a monstrous hunting bird that chased after mammals such as this early horse.

PREHISTORIC LIFE

83 **The largest land mammal ever to have lived was a type of rhino—without a nose horn.** *Paraceratherium* was far bigger than an elephant, at 26 feet long and 20 feet tall at the shoulder. It weighed over 16 tons—more than three elephants. This giant creature lived in Asia about 30 million years ago and was a peaceful plant-eater.

84 **Giant marsupials may have been the origin of stories of the "Bunyip," a mythical Australian animal.** The Bunyip was supposed to live in swamps and waterholes, and its name means "devil" in native Australian mythology.

▲ The huge *Paraceratherium* fed by browsing on trees, stripping off the leaves. Even though it was so big and heavy, *Paraceratherium* had long legs, which means it was probably capable of running.

Our prehistoric relations

85 Monkeys, apes, and humans first appeared over 50 million years ago—the first kinds looked like squirrels. This group is called the primates. *Plesiadapis* was an early primate. It lived 55 million years ago in Europe and North America.

◀ *Plesiadapis* had claws on its fingers and toes, unlike monkeys and apes, which had nails.

86 Early apes walked on all fours. About 20 million years ago, *Dryopithecus* lived in Europe and Asia. It used its arms and legs to climb trees. When it came down to the ground, it walked on all fours. It was 2 feet long and ate fruit and leaves.

87 Some kinds of apes may have walked on their two back legs, like us. About 4.5 million years ago *Ardipithecus* lived in Africa. Only a few of its fossils have been found. However, experts think it may have walked upright on its back legs. It could have made the first steps in the change, or evolution, from apes to humans.

◀ The early ape *Dryopithecus* walked flat on its feet, unlike other apes, which walked on their knuckles.

PREHISTORIC LIFE

88 The first fossils of a giant prehistoric ape were found in a pharmacy shop in Hong Kong, more than 70 years ago. They were discovered by a German scientist in 1935, who named the ape *Gigantopithecus* from just a few fossil teeth.

89 *Gigantopithecus* really was a giant—it was more than 10 feet tall! Its name, *Gigantopithecus*, means "giant ape." It was much larger than today's biggest ape, the gorilla, which grows up to 6.5 feet tall. *Gigantopithecus* probably ate roots and seeds, and may have hunted small animals such as birds, rats, and lizards.

▲ The need to see longer distances on grasslands may have caused the first apes to walk on two legs.

▶ The enormous *Gigantopithecus* could probably stand on its hind legs to reach food.

90 Scientists work out which animals are our closest cousins partly from fossils—and also from chemicals. The chemical called DNA contains genes, which are instructions for how living things grow and work. The living animals with DNA most similar to ours are the great apes, chimpanzees and gorillas, both from Africa. So our ancient cousins were probably apes like them. The orangutan, from Southeast Asia, is less similar.

DINOSAURS

91 **For more than 160 million years, dinosaurs ruled the land.** There were many different kinds—huge and tiny, tall and short, slim and bulky, fast and slow, with fierce sharp-toothed meat-eaters and peacefully munching plant-eaters. Then a great disaster ended their rule.

▼ In South America 70 million years ago, a group of *Austroraptor* dinosaurs attack a huge plant-eater. Many fast, fierce "raptor" dinosaurs had feathers. *Austroraptor* was one of the largest raptors at 660-plus pounds and 16 feet long.

When were dinosaurs alive?

92 The Age of Dinosaurs lasted from about 230 million to 65 million years ago, during a time called the Mesozoic Era. Dinosaurs were the main creatures on land for 80 times longer than people have been on Earth!

▼ Toward the end of the Paleozoic Era, reptiles replaced amphibians as the main large land animals. Dinosaurs were in turn replaced in the Cenozoic Era by mammals. MYA means million years ago.

93 Dinosaurs were not the only animals living in the Mesozoic Era. There were many other kinds such as insects, spiders, shellfish, fish, scurrying lizards, crocodiles, and furry mammals.

94 There were different shapes and sizes of dinosaurs. Some were small enough to hold in your hand. Others were bigger than a house!

◀ Tiny *Saltopus*, less than 3 feet long, was a Triassic close cousin of dinosaurs.

PALEOZOIC ERA

The reptiles, including the ancestors of the dinosaurs, start to become more dominant than the amphibians.

Lystrosaurus (amphibian)

Diplocaulus (mammal-like reptile)

**299–251 MYA
PERMIAN PERIOD**

MESOZOIC ERA

The first true dinosaurs appear. These are small two-legged carnivores (meat-eaters), and larger herbivores, or plant-eaters.

Procompsognathus

Riojasaurus

**251–200 MYA
TRIASSIC PERIOD**

Many different dinosaurs lived at this time, including the giant plant-eaters such as *Barosaurus*.

Barosaurus

Allosaurus

**200–145.5 MYA
JURASSIC PERIOD**

DINOSAURS

◀ *Stegosaurus* thrived during the late Jurassic Period, in North America and Europe.

96 There were no people during the Age of Dinosaurs. There was a gap of more than 60 million years between the last dinosaurs and the first humans.

I DON'T BELIEVE IT!
The name "dinosaur" means "terrible lizard." But dinosaurs weren't lizards, and not all dinosaurs were terrible. Small plant-eating dinosaurs were about as terrible as today's sheep!

95 No single kind of dinosaur survived for all of the Mesozoic Era. Many different types came and went. Some lasted for less than a million years. Other kinds, like *Stegosaurus*, kept going for many millions of years.

MESOZOIC ERA

During the last part of the Age of Dinosaurs, both giant carnivores and armored herbivores were alive.

Tyrannosaurus rex
Deinonychus
Saltasaurus
Spinosaurus

**145.5–65.5 MYA
CRETACEOUS PERIOD**

CENOZOIC ERA

The dinosaurs have died out, and large mammals soon take over the land.

Megacerops
herbivorous mammal

**65.5–23 MYA
PALEOGENE PERIOD**

Newer kinds of mammals become more common, such as cats, horses, whales, and bats.

Thylacosmilus
carnivorous mammal

Nesodon
herbivorous mammal

**23–2.6 MYA
NEOGENE PERIOD**

Before the dinosaurs

97 Dinosaurs were not the first animals on Earth. Many other kinds of creatures lived before them, including different types of reptiles—the group that includes dinosaurs.

▶ *Erythrosuchus* was a crocodilelike reptile that lived before dinosaurs were common.

98 *Dimetrodon* was a fierce, meat-eating reptile. Although it looked like a dinosaur it wasn't one. It lived 270 million years ago, well before the dinosaurs arrived. *Dimetrodon* was about 10 feet long and had a tall flap of skin like a sail on its back.

▶ *Dimetrodon*'s legs sprawled sideways from its body, like a lizard, rather than being underneath, as in dinosaurs.

99 Early crocodiles also looked rather like dinosaurs. Crocodiles were around before the first dinosaurs. One was *Erythrosuchus*, which was 15 feet long, lived 240 million years ago, lurked in swamps, and ate fish.

DINOSAURS

100 Therapsids were around before the dinosaurs, and they also lived alongside the early dinosaurs. They were mammal-like reptiles because they didn't have scaly skin like most reptiles. Instead they had furry or hairy skin like mammals.

101 The dinosaur group probably appeared 238–232 million years ago. Lack of fossils means no one is sure when, where, or what were the ancestors. However it is known that the dinosaurs' closest relations include crocodiles and the flying reptiles called pterosaurs, all making up the bigger group termed archosaurs.

▶ *Euparkeria* could probably rear up to run on just its two rear legs—like many meat-eating dinosaurs later.

102 Some small reptiles show what the dinosaurs' ancestors could have looked like. They include *Euparkeria* in South Africa 245 million years ago, and *Lagosuchus* and *Marasuchus* in South America around 235 million years ago. They were small, light, and fast, with long back legs, and sharp teeth for feeding on bugs and small creatures.

QUIZ

1. Did *Dimetrodon* live before or after the dinosaurs?
2. Did therapsids have scaly or furry skin?
3. What were the flying reptiles related to dinosaurs known as?
4. Did dinosaurs gradually change, or evolve into crocodiles?

Answers:
1. Before 2. Furry skin 3. Pterosaurs 4. Dinosaurs did not evolve into crocodiles, dinosaurs appeared afterward

Dinosaurs arrive

103 **The earliest dinosaurs stalked the Earth almost 230 million years ago.** They lived in what is now Argentina, in South America. They included *Eoraptor* and *Herrerasaurus*. Both were slim and fast creatures. They could stand almost upright and run on their two rear legs. Few other animals of the time could run upright like this, on legs that were straight below their bodies. Most other animals had legs that stuck out sideways.

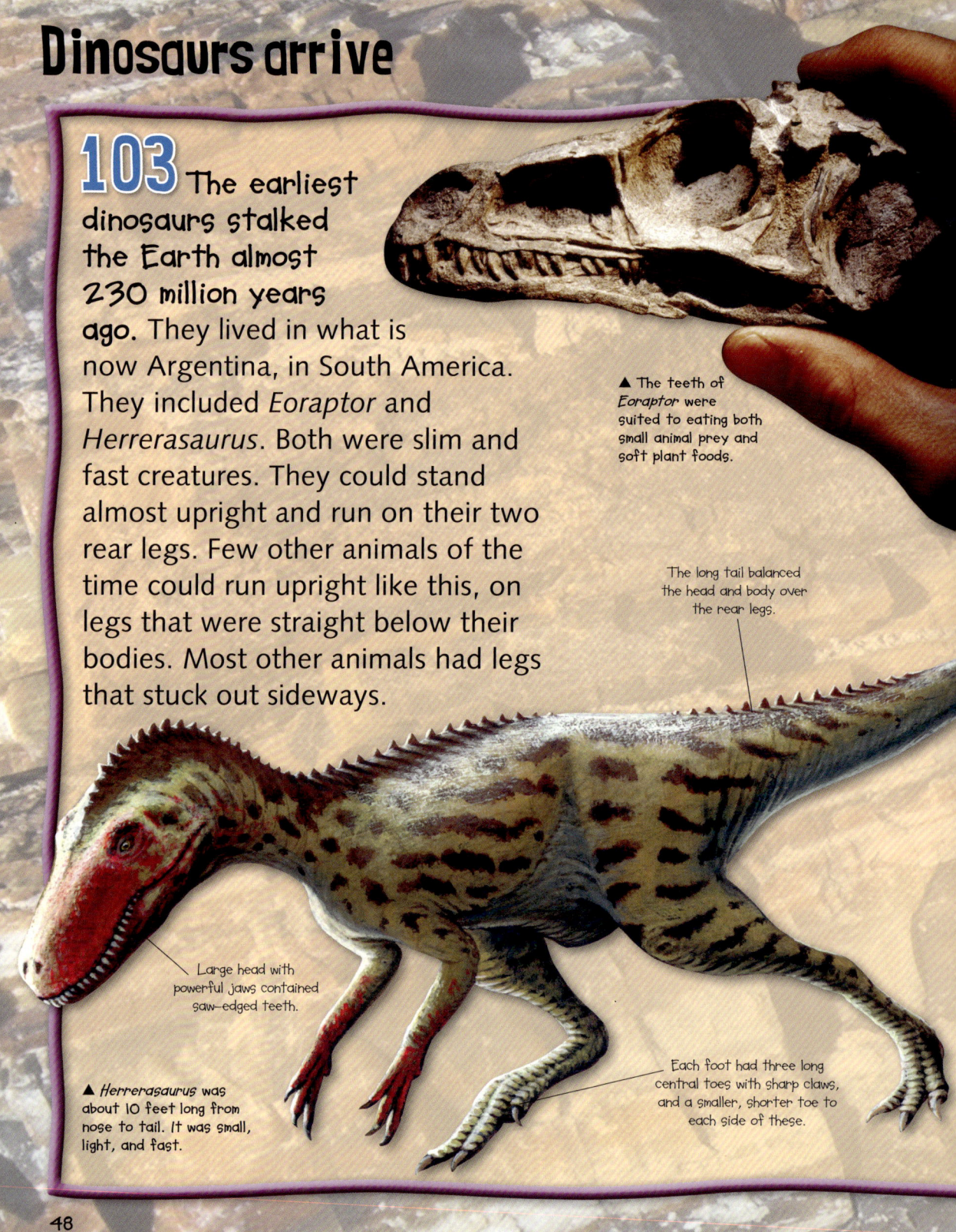

▲ The teeth of *Eoraptor* were suited to eating both small animal prey and soft plant foods.

The long tail balanced the head and body over the rear legs.

Large head with powerful jaws contained saw-edged teeth.

▲ *Herrerasaurus* was about 10 feet long from nose to tail. It was small, light, and fast.

Each foot had three long central toes with sharp claws, and a smaller, shorter toe to each side of these.

DINOSAURS

104 Early dinosaurs hunted small animals such as lizards and other reptiles, insects, and worms. They had lightweight bodies and long, strong legs to chase after prey. Their claws were long and sharp for grabbing victims. Their large mouths were filled with pointed teeth to bite and tear up their food.

▶ One of the early big dinosaurs, 2-ton *Lessemasaurus* lived about 210 million years ago in South America.

105 As early dinosaurs spread over the land they began to change, or evolve, into new kinds. Evolution has happened in all living things since life began. New kinds of plants and animals appeared, thrived for a time, and then died out. Some of the early dinosaurs evolved to be much bigger and eat plants, like 30-foot-long *Lessemasaurus*.

STRONG LEGS!

You will need:
cardboard   sticky tape   safe scissors   split pins

1. Copy the picture of *Herrerasaurus* on page 48 onto cardboard, without the rear legs. Color it in on both sides and cut it out with help from an adult.
2. On another piece of cardboard, copy the rear legs, color them in, and cut them out.
3. Fix the legs to the body, either side of the hip area, with the split pins. Adjust the angle of the body over the legs. This is how many dinosaurs stood and walked.

First of the giants

106 One of the first big dinosaurs well-known from fossils was *Plateosaurus*. This plant-eater grew up to 26 feet long and lived almost 220 million years ago in what is now Europe. It could rear up on its back legs and use its long neck to reach food high in trees.

Long, flexible neck for reaching food high off the ground

Sharp, jabbing claws for defense

Long, strong tail for balance

Powerful back legs for rearing up

▲ Fossils of more than 100 *Plateosaurus* have been found, so its size, shape, teeth, and body details are well known compared to many other dinosaurs.

DINOSAURS

107 *Riojasaurus* was an even larger plant-eater. It lived 218 million years ago in what is now Argentina. *Riojasaurus* was 32 feet long and weighed over one ton—as much as a large family car of today.

Small head and long, flexible neck

108 The first big plant-eating dinosaurs may have become larger, with longer necks, so that they could reach up into trees for food. Their great size would also have helped them fight enemies, since many other big meat-eating reptiles, some as long as 16 feet, were ready to make a meal of them.

◀ Like *Plateosaurus*, *Riojasaurus* was in the dinosaur group called prosauropods, with a small head, long neck, and long tail.

109 These early dinosaurs lived during the first part of the Age of Dinosaurs—the Triassic Period. By its end, 200 million years ago, dozens of kinds of dinosaurs roamed across much of the world.

I DON'T BELIEVE IT!

Early plant-eating dinosaurs did not eat fruits or grasses—there weren't any! They hadn't appeared yet. Instead they ate plants called horsetails, ferns, cycads, and conifer trees.

What teeth tell us

110 We know about dinosaurs and other living things from long ago because of fossils. These are usually hard body parts, such as bones, claws, horns, and scales, that are preserved in rocks for millions of years. Dinosaur teeth were very hard and formed many fossils.

112 The shape of a dinosaur's teeth help to show what it ate. *Edmontosaurus* was a 40-foot-long duck-billed dinosaur, and had rows of broad, wide, sharp-ridged teeth in the sides of its mouth. These were ideal for chewing tough plant foods like twigs and old leaves.

◄ The head of *Edmontosaurus* was long, broad, and muscular, suited to spending hours chewing—similar to today's horse.

Toothless beaklike front of mouth

More than 500 chewing back teeth

111 *Tyrannosaurus* had 50–60 long, pointed teeth more than 8 inches long. These were excellent for tearing up victims, and for ripping off lumps of flesh for swallowing. As in other dinosaurs, all through life as old teeth broke or fell out, new ones grew in their place.

► *Tyrannosaurus* teeth were strong and stout, but not especially sharp-edged, more suited to tearing than slicing.

113 Some dinosaurs, such as *Gallimimus*, had no teeth at all! The mouth was shaped like a bird's beak and made of a tough, strong, horny substance like our fingernails. The beak was suited to pecking up all kinds of foods like seeds, worms, and bugs, as many birds do today.

▲ *Gallimimus* was a type of "ostrich dinosaur" with large eyes, a long, lightweight beak, and long neck.

114 *Baryonyx* had narrow, pointed, cone-shaped teeth. These resemble the teeth of a crocodile or dolphin today. They were ideal for grabbing slippery prey such as fish.

▲ The head of *Baryonyx* was more than 3 feet long, with an expanded, spoon-shaped front snout.

115 The teeth of the giant, long-necked dinosaur *Apatosaurus* were shaped like pencils. They worked like a rake to pull leaves off branches into the mouth, for the dinosaur to swallow.

DINOSAUR TEETH!

With the help of an adult, look in a utensils drawer or tool box for dinosaur teeth! Some tools resemble the teeth of some dinosaurs, and do similar jobs.
File: broad surface with hard ridges, like the plant-chewing teeth of *Edmontosaurus*.
Knife: long and pointed, like the meat-tearing teeth of *Tyrannosaurus rex*.
Pliers: Gripping and squeezing, like the beak-shaped mouth of *Gallimimus*.

▲ Although *Apatosaurus* was about 82 feet long, its skull measured just 23 inches. It spent most of its time feeding.

Supersize dinosaurs

116 **The true giants of the Age of Dinosaurs were the sauropods.** These vast dinosaurs all had a small head, long neck, barrel-shaped body, long tapering tail, and four pillarlike legs. The biggest sauropods included *Brachiosaurus*, *Mamenchisaurus*, *Barosaurus*, *Diplodocus*, *Futalognkosaurus*, and *Argentinosaurus*.

◀ Fossil footprints from a sauropod herd near Purgatoire River, Colorado.

117 **Sauropod dinosaurs probably lived in groups or herds.** We know this from their footprints, which have been preserved as fossils. Each foot left a print as large as a chair seat. Hundreds of footprints together showed many sauropods walked along with each other.

DINOSAURS

▲ *Futalognkosaurus*, a type of sauropod known as a titanosaur, was more than 100 feet long. Its name, given in 2007, means "giant chief lizard" in the local Argentinian language.

118 *Diplodocus* is also known as "Old Whiptail!" It may have swished its long tail so hard and fast that it made an enormous crack like a whip. This living, leathery, scaly whip would scare away enemies or even rip off their skin.

119 Sauropod dinosaurs swallowed pebbles—on purpose! Their peglike teeth could only rake in plant food, not chew it. Pebbles and stones gulped into the stomach helped to grind and crush the food. These pebbles, smooth and polished by the grinding, have been found with the fossil bones of sauropods.

▶ *Brachiosaurus* was about 80 feet long and probably weighed more than 30 tons. Its amazingly long neck allowed it to browse from the tallest trees.

120 The biggest sauropods like *Brachiosaurus* and *Futalognkosaurus* were enormous beasts. They weighed up to ten times more than elephants of today. Yet their fossil footprints showed they could run quite fast—nearly as quickly as you!

121 Sauropods probably had to eat most of the time, 20 hours out of every 24. They had enormous bodies that would need great amounts of food, but only small mouths to gather the food.

Killer claws

122 Nearly all dinosaurs had claws on their fingers and toes. These claws were shaped for different jobs in different dinosaurs. They were made from a tough substance called keratin—the same as your fingernails and toenails.

123 *Hypsilophodon* had strong, sturdy claws. This small 6.5-foot-long plant-eater probably used them to scrabble and dig in soil for seeds and roots.

124 *Deinonychus* had long, hooked claws on its hands. These helped it to grab victims and tear at their skin and flesh. It also had a huge hooked claw, as big as your hand, on the second toe of each foot. This could flick down like a pointed knife to slash pieces out of prey.

◀ *Deinonychus*, meaning "terrible claw," probably had feathers like other raptors. It lived in North America 110 million years ago.

Long claw on each of the three fingers

Second toe had slashing "terrible claw"

DINOSAURS

125 *Baryonyx* also had a large claw, but this was on the thumb of each hand. It may have worked as a fish-hook to snatch fish from water.

126 *Iguanodon* had claws on its feet. But these were rounded and blunt and looked more like hooves. There were also stubby claws on the fingers, while the thumb claw was longer and shaped like a spike, perhaps for stabbing enemies.

▶ Therizinosaurs, from the Cretaceous Period in Eastern Asia and Western North America, had enormous finger claws—why is a mystery.

127 Giant sauropod dinosaurs had almost flat claws. Dinosaurs such as *Apatosaurus* looked like they had toenails on their huge feet!

▶ The long claw on *Apatosaurus*' front foot was possibly for self defense.

128 The biggest claws of any dinosaurs, and any animals, belonged to the scythe dinosaurs or therizinosaurs. Their hand claws, up to 3 feet long, were perhaps used to pull down and cut off leafy branches as food.

129 Therizinosaurs were big, strange-looking dinosaurs, reaching 32 feet long and weighing more than 5 tons. They lived late in the Age of Dinosaurs, and the group included *Alxasaurus*, *Nothronychus*, *Beipiaosaurus*, and *Therizinosaurus*.

Deadly meat-eaters

Spinosaurus lived about 100 million years ago. It grew to 50 feet in length, and weighed as much as 11 tons.

About 40 feet in length, *Carcharodontosaurus* hunted across North Africa 95 million years ago. Its saw-edged teeth were 8 inches long.

Giganotosaurus was up to 45 feet long and had the largest skull of any meat-eating dinosaur. It lived about 97 million years ago.

130 **The biggest meat-eating dinosaurs were the largest predators ever to walk on Earth.** *Allosaurus*, which lived 150 million years ago in North America, reached almost 30 feet in length, while *Tyrannosaurus rex* from 66 million years ago was around 40 feet. In South America, *Giganotosaurus* was slightly larger, while in North Africa, *Carcharodontosaurus* and *Spinosaurus* were even bigger—the largest meat-eating dinosaurs known so far.

I DON'T BELIEVE IT!
Some meat-eating dinosaurs not only bit their prey, but also each other! Fossils of several *Tyrannosaurus* had bite marks on the head. Perhaps they fought each other to become chief in the group, like wolves do today.

131 These great predators were well equipped for hunting large prey—including other dinosaurs. They had massive mouths with long sharp teeth in powerful jaws. They also had long, strong back legs to run fast, and enormous toe claws for kicking and holding down victims.

132 Meat-eaters probably got food in various ways. They hid behind rocks or trees and rushed out to surprise a victim. Some chased their prey, and others would plod steadily over time to tire out their meal. They might even scavenge—feast on the bodies of creatures that were dead or dying from old age, illness, or injury.

T-Rex was among the last of the great predatory dinosaurs. It probably weighed around 7 tons when fully grown.

Allosaurus was the largest meat-eating dinosaur of the Jurassic Period. It was a relative lightweight at only 2–3 tons!

Look! Listen! Sniff!

133 **Like the reptiles of today, dinosaurs could see, hear, and smell the world around them.** We know this from fossils. The preserved fossil skulls had spaces for eyes, ears, and nostrils.

134 **Some dinosaurs, such as *Leaellynasaura* and *Troodon*, had big eyes.** There are large, bowl-shaped hollows in their fossil skulls to allow for them. Today, animals such as mice, owls, and night-time lizards can see well in the dark. Perhaps *Troodon* prowled through the forest at night, peering in the gloom for small creatures to eat.

▶ *Troodon* was about 6.5 feet long and lived in North America 70 million years ago.

▶ *Leaellynasaura*, was a 10-foot-long plant-eater from 115 million years ago in what is now Australia.

135 **There are also spaces on the sides of the head where *Troodon* had its ears.** Dinosaur ears were round and flat, like the ears of other reptiles. *Troodon* could hear the tiny noises of little animals moving about in the dark.

136 The nostrils of *Troodon*, where it breathed in air and smelled scents, were two holes at the front of its snout. With its delicate sense of smell, *Troodon* could sniff out its prey of insects, worms, little reptiles such as lizards, and small shrewlike mammals.

BIG EYES

You will need:
stiff cardboard   safe scissors   elastic   color pencils

1. Make a cardboard *Troodon* mask. With help from an adult, cut out the shape as shown. Then cut out two small eye holes, each 0.4 inches across.
2. Color in your mask, and attach elastic so you can wear it.
3. Put on your mask. How much can you see when wearing it?
4. Make the eye holes as large as the eyes of the real *Troodon*. Now you can have a much bigger, clearer view of the world!

137 Dinosaurs used their eyes, ears, and noses not only to find food, but also to detect enemies—and each other. *Parasaurolophus* had a long, hollow, tubelike crest on its head. Perhaps it blew air along this to make a noise like a trumpet, as an elephant does today with its trunk.

138 Dinosaurs such as *Parasaurolophus* may have made noises to send messages to other members of their group or herd. Different messages could tell the others about finding food or warn them about enemies.

▼ *Parasaurolophus* was a "duck-billed" dinosaur or hadrosaur. It was about 32 feet long and lived 80 million years ago in North America.

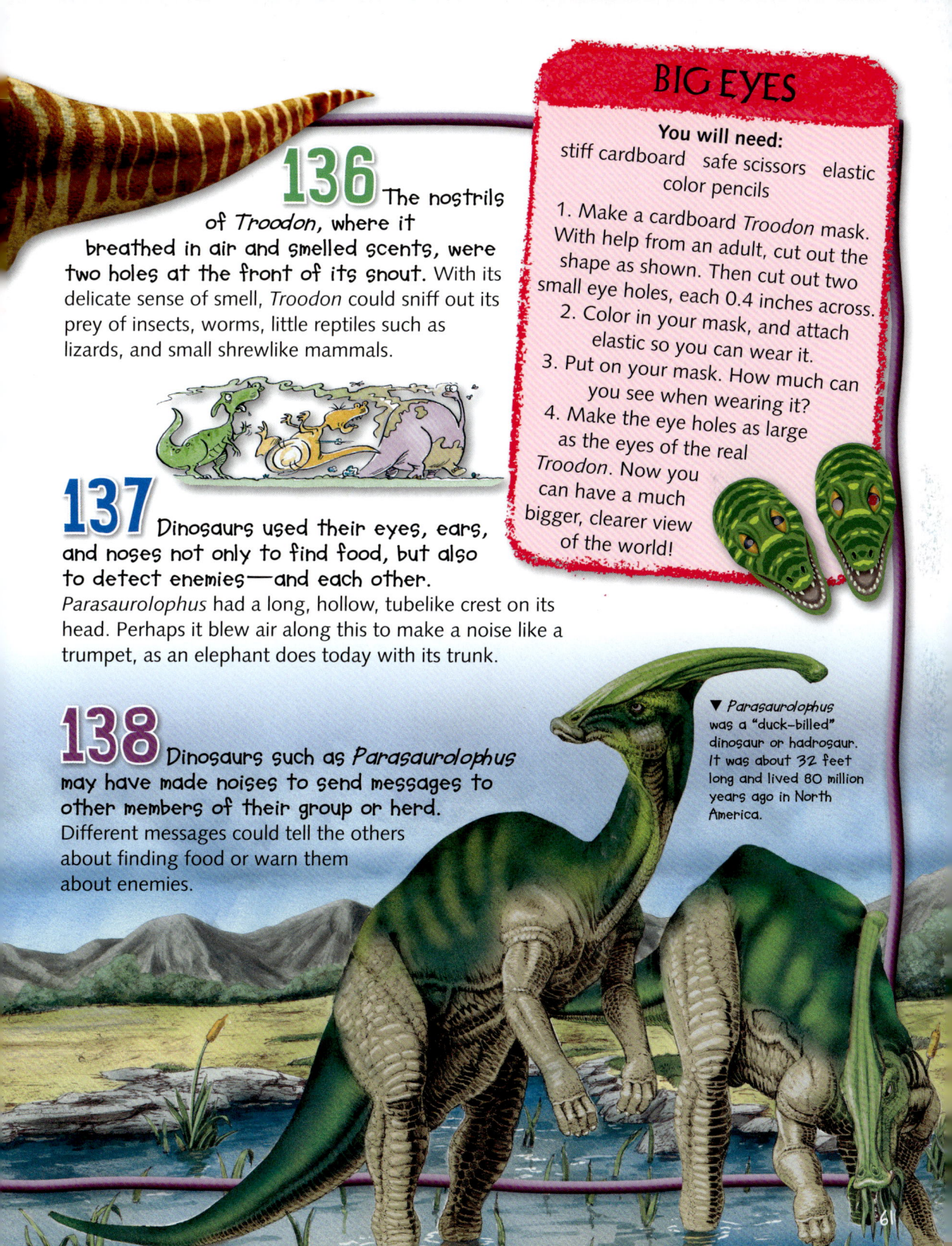

Living with dinosaurs

139 All dinosaurs walked and ran on land, as far as we know. No dinosaurs could fly in the air or spend their lives swimming in the water. But many other creatures, which lived at the same time as the dinosaurs, could fly or swim. Some were reptiles, like the dinosaurs.

140 Ichthyosaurs were reptiles that lived in the sea. They were shaped like dolphins, long and slim with fins and a tail. They chased after fish to eat.

141 Plesiosaurs were sea-dwelling reptiles. They had long necks, rounded bodies, four large flippers, and a short tail.

142 Turtles were another kind of reptile that swam in the oceans long ago. Each had a strong, domed shell and four flippers. Turtles still survive today. However ichthyosaurs and then plesiosaurs died out by the end of the Age of Dinosaurs.

▶ In this marine and shoreline Cretaceous scene, the dinosaurs *Ouranosaurus* (4) are shown living alongside lots of other types of animals.

143 **Pterosaurs were reptiles that could fly.** They had thin, skinlike wings held out by long finger bones. Some soared over the sea and grabbed small fish in their sharp-toothed, beak-shaped mouths. Others swooped on small land animals.

144 **Birds first appeared about 150 million years ago.** Some evolved to dive for fish in the sea, like gulls and terns today. *Ichthyornis* was about 10 inches long and lived along North American coasts.

▲ Unlike modern birds, *Ichthyornis* had tiny teeth in its jaws to grip slippery prey.

Key
1 *Hesperornis* (flightless bird)
2 *Elasmosaurus* (marine reptile)
3 *Pteranodon* (flying reptile)
4 *Ouranosaurus* (dinosaur)
5 *Archelon* (turtle, laying eggs)
6 *Archelon* (turtle, swimming)
7 *Kronosaurus* (marine reptile)
8 *Ichthyosaurus* (marine reptile)
9 Belemnoid (mollusk, similar to modern squid)
10 *Mosasaurus* (marine reptile)
11 *Elasmosaurus* (marine reptile)
12 Ammonoid (mollusk)
13 *Cretoxyrhina* (shark)

145 **Mosasaurs were huge, fearsome reptiles that appeared later in the Age of Dinosaurs.** Related to lizards, they had a massive mouth full of sharp teeth. Some grew to 43 feet long and weighed over 5 tons.

How fast?

146 Dinosaurs walked and ran at different speeds, according to their size and shape. In the world today, cheetahs and ostriches are slim with long legs and run very fast. Elephants and hippos are huge heavyweights and plod along more slowly. Dinosaurs were similar. Some were big, heavy, and slow. Others were slim, light, and speedy.

QUIZ

Put these dinosaurs and modern animals in order of top running speed, from slow to fast.
Human (25 miles an hour)
Cheetah (60-plus miles an hour)
Muttaburrasaurus (9 miles an hour)
Ornithomimus (43 miles an hour)
Sloth (0.1 miles an hour)
Coelophysis (18 miles an hour)

Answer:
Sloth, Muttaburrasaurus, Coelophysis, Human, Ornithomimus, Cheetah

▼ *Ornithomimus*, from North America 70–65 million years ago, had long, powerful back legs, and hollow bones (like a bird) to save weight.

147 The fastest dinosaurs were the ostrich dinosaurs, or ornithomimosaurs. They had a similar body shape and proportions to today's biggest and fastest-running bird, the ostrich. *Ornithomimus* was one of the largest, up to 16 feet long and 660 pounds in weight.

148
Muttaburrasaurus was a huge ornithopod type of dinosaur, a cousin of Iguanodon. It probably walked about as fast as you, around 2 to 3 miles an hour. It might have been able to gallop along at a top speed of 9 miles an hour, making the ground shake with its 3-ton weight!

▶ Fossils of *Muttaburrasaurus* come from Queensland, Australia. This bulky plant-eater had three large toes on each back foot and also three on the smaller front foot.

Ankle bones

Foot bones

Toe bones ended in rounded claws

149
Coelophysis was a slim, lightweight dinosaur. It could probably trot, jump, and dart about with great agility. Sometimes it ran upright on its two back legs. Or it could bound along on all fours like a dog at more than 18 miles an hour.

▼ *Coelophysis* was 10 feet long. It was one of the earliest dinosaurs, living about 220 million years ago.

Built like tanks

150 Some dinosaurs had body defenses against predators. These might be large horns and spikes, or thick, hard lumps of bone like armor-plating. Most armored dinosaurs were plant-eaters. They had to defend themselves against big meat-eating dinosaurs such as *Tyrannosaurus rex*.

151 *Triceratops* had three horns, one on its nose and two much longer ones above its eyes. It also had a wide shieldlike piece of bone over its neck and shoulders. The horns and neck frill made *Triceratops* look very fearsome. But most of the time it quietly ate plants. If attacked, *Triceratops* could charge and jab with its horns, like a rhino today.

▼ *Triceratops* was 30 feet long and weighed more than 5 tons. It lived 65 million years ago in North America.

- Wide neck frill of bone and skin
- Long, sharp brow horns
- Smaller nose horn
- Sharp beak-shaped front of mouth
- Wide feet spread great body weight

152 *Styracosaurus* was a ceratopsian ("horn-face") dinosaur, like *Triceratops*, but with a more elaborate neck frill. Up to six horns as long as 3 feet extended from the frill's edge, giving this dinosaur an even fiercer appearance.

DESIGN A DINOSAUR!

Make an imaginary dinosaur. It might have the body armor and tail club of *Euoplocephalus*, or the head horns and neck frill of *Triceratops*. You can draw your dinosaur, or make it out of pieces of card or from modeling clay. Give it a made-up name, like *Euoploceratops* or *Tricephalus*. How well protected is your dinosaur? How does it compare to some armored creatures of today, such as tortoises, armadillos, or porcupines?

Tail club made from several fused (joined) bones

Long, straight, powerful tail to swing club

▲ *Styracosaurus* grew up to 20 feet long and was 6 feet tall at the shoulder.

Back covered with bony plates set within the skin

153 *Euoplocephalus* had a great lump of bone on its tail. This measured almost 3 feet across and looked like a massive hammer or club. *Euoplocephalus* could swing it at predators to protect itself from attack.

◀ *Euoplocephalus* belonged to the group called ankylosaurs. With big bony sheets and lumps in their skin, they were the most armored of all dinosaurs.

Nests and eggs

154 Like most reptiles today, dinosaurs produced young by laying eggs. These hatched out into baby dinosaurs that gradually grew into adults.

155 Many kinds of dinosaur eggs and babies have been found. These include those of small, strong-beaked *Oviraptor* from Central Asia and the early sauropod *Massospondylus* from South Africa.

156 Different dinosaurs laid different sizes and shapes of eggs. Huge sauropod dinosaurs such as *Brachiosaurus* probably laid rounded eggs as big as basketballs. Eggs of big meat-eaters like *Tyrannosaurus* were more sausage-shaped, 15 inches long and 5 inches wide.

157 Some dinosaurs made nests for their eggs. *Oviraptor* lived more than 75 million years ago in what is now the Gobi Desert of Asia. It probably scraped a bowl-shaped nest in the soil about 3 feet across. Into this it laid about 15–20 eggs, in a neat spiral shape.

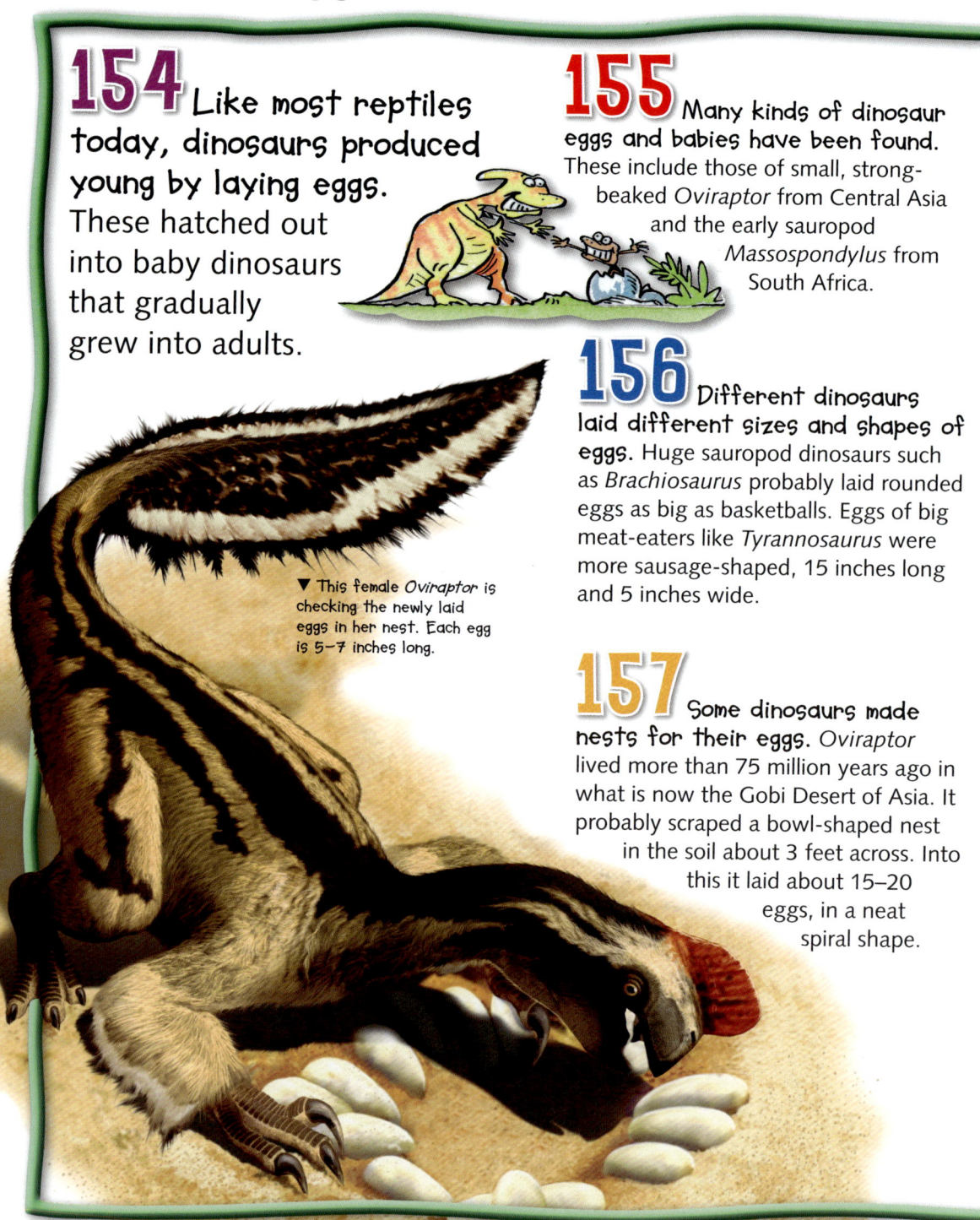

▼ This female *Oviraptor* is checking the newly laid eggs in her nest. Each egg is 5–7 inches long.

DINOSAURS

158 Dinosaur eggs probably hatched after a few weeks or months, depending on how warm it was. The eggshells were slightly leathery and bendy, like most reptile eggshells today, and not brittle or hard like the shells of modern birds' eggs.

▲ Studying preserved unhatched eggs (real fossil, left) shows they contained tiny baby dinosaurs (artist's drawing, right).

▶ Seventy-five million years ago in East Asia, pig-sized *Protoceratops* prepares to defend its nest and eggs from a hungry *Velociraptor*.

159 Fossils of baby dinosaurs show that they looked very much like their parents. However the neck frill of a baby *Protoceratops* was not as large when compared to the rest of its body, as in the adult. As the youngster's body grew, the frill grew faster, so its relative size changed. Other dinosaurs' body proportions also changed as they grew bigger.

160 Recent fossil finds show that some dinosaurs looked after their babies, like some reptiles today, such as crocodiles. In one discovery, an adult *Protoceratops* was preserved with some babies just 4–6 inches long, probably less than one year old.

Dinosaur babies

161 **Some dinosaur parents may have fed their young.** Fossils of duck-billed *Maiasaura* include nests, eggs, and newly hatched young. The hatchlings could not move around because their leg bones were not strong enough. Yet their tiny teeth had slight scratches and other marks from eating food. So the parent *Maiasaura* probably brought food, such as leaves and berries, to the nest for them.

▼ In 1978 more than 200 fossils of *Maiasaura* nests, eggs, babies, youngsters, and adults were found at a site now known as "Egg Mountain" in Montana. They date to around 75 million years ago.

▲ *Maiasaura* was a 30-foot-long plant-eater belonging to the hadrosaur group. Its newly hatched babies were only 15 inches long, but within a year they had grown to 5 feet.

162 **The nest of *Maiasaura* was a mud mound about 6.5 feet across, with 30–40 eggs and babies.** Some fossils show unhatched eggs broken into many small parts, as though squashed by the babies that had already hatched out.

DINOSAURS

163 Baby dinosaurs grew up to five times faster than human babies. A baby sauropod dinosaur like *Diplodocus* was already 3 feet long and 18 pounds in weight when it hatched from its egg!

164 Some dinosaurs may even have cared for their young after they left the nest. *Psittacosaurus* was a 6.5-foot-long plant-eater that lived 130–100 million years ago in East Asia. One set of fossils from China suggests that one adult was guarding 34 babies when they all died together, perhaps because the tunnel they were hiding in collapsed.

▼ Fossils of *Psittacosaurus* found in 2003 suggest that one adult may have looked after more than 30 babies.

The end for the dinosaurs

165 **About 65 million years ago, the Age of Dinosaurs came to a sudden end.** Fossils preserved in the rocks show great changes at this time. However the fossils also show that creatures like fish, insects, birds, and mammals carried on. What happened to kill off some of the biggest, most successful animals the world has ever seen? There are many ideas. It could have been one disaster, or a combination of several.

DINOSAURS

166 The disaster may have been caused by a giant lump of rock, an asteroid or meteorite. This came from outer space and smashed into the Earth. The impact threw up vast clouds of water, rocks, ash, and dust that blotted out the Sun for many years. Plants could not grow in the gloom, so many plant-eating dinosaurs died. This meant meat-eaters had less food, so they died as well.

167 Many volcanoes around the Earth could have erupted all at the same time, perhaps due to the meteorite impact. They threw out red-hot rocks, ash, dust, and poison gas. Creatures would have choked and died in the gloom.

▼ Scientific studies show that 65.5 million years ago, a space rock smashed into Earth near what is now Yucatan, Mexico.

168 The disaster might have involved a terrible disease. Perhaps this gradually spread among certain kinds of animals and killed them off.

METEORITE SMASH!

You will need:
plastic bowl   flour   large pebble   desk lamp

Put the flour in the bowl. This is Earth's surface. Place the desk lamp so it shines over the top of the bowl. This is the Sun. The pebble is the meteorite from space. Drop the pebble into the bowl. See how the tiny bits of flour float in the air like a mist, making the "Sun" dimmer. A real meteorite smash may have been the beginning of the end for the great dinosaurs.

169 It might be that dinosaur eggs were eaten by a plague of animals. Small, shrewlike mammals were around at the time. They may have eaten the eggs at night as the dinosaurs slept.

What happened next?

170 Other kinds of animals died out with dinosaurs. Flying reptiles called pterosaurs, and swimming reptiles called mosasaurs and plesiosaurs, disappeared. Lots of plants died out too. When a group of living things dies out, it is called an extinction. When many groups disappear at the same time, it's known as a mass extinction.

172 Even though many kinds of animals and plants died out 65 million years ago, other groups lived on. Crabs, shellfish, insects, worms, fish, frogs, and mammals all survived the mass extinction—and these groups are still alive today.

171 Several groups of reptiles also survived the mass extinction. They include crocodiles and alligators, turtles and tortoises, lizards, and snakes. Why some kinds died out in the great disaster, yet other types survived, is one of the main puzzles that experts today are still trying to solve.

Key
1. *Coryphodon* (browsing mammal)
2. *Gastornis* (flightless bird)
3. *Eobasileus* (browsing mammal)
4. *Branisella* (early monkey)
5. *Tremacebus* (early monkey)
6. *Paraceratherium* (browsing mammal)
7. *Arsinoitherium* (browsing mammal)
8. *Hyracotherium* (early horse)
9. *Andrewsarchus* (carnivorous mammal)
10. *Eobasileus* (browsing mammal)
11. *Plesiadapis* (early primate)
12. *Ptilodus* (squirrel-like mammal)
13. *Chriacus* (raccoonlike mammal)

DINOSAURS

173 **After the mass extinction, a different group of animals began to take over the land.** These were the mammals. Through the Age of Dinosaurs they were mostly small and skulking, coming out only after dark. Now they could change or evolve to become bigger. Within a few million years they had developed into many kinds, from peaceful plant-eaters to huge, fierce predators.

▼ The mass extinction of 65 million years ago killed big dinosaurs and many other kinds of animals and plants. But plenty of animals survived, especially the mammals.

75

T-REX

174 Almost everyone has heard of *Tyrannosaurus rex*. Wasn't it the biggest dinosaur of all time, the greatest meat-eater with a mouth big enough to swallow a car and teeth as long as swords? Not one of these "facts" is true. Certainly *Tyrannosaurus rex* is one of the world's most famous animals. Even though it died out 65 million years ago, it "lives on" in movies, toys and games, as statues and works of art, and in music and songs. However, *Tyrannosaurus rex* is also the subject of many mistaken beliefs.

▶ A scene from the 2005 movie *King Kong*. With a mighty roar *Tyrannosaurus rex* bares its huge mouth filled with sharp teeth and prepares to attack. Images like this are familiar—but are they correct? For example, did T-Rex really roar loudly?

Terror of its age

▲ The last dinosaurs of the Late Cretaceous Period ranged from small, speedy hunters such as *Avimimus* to giant plant-eaters, three-horned *Triceratops*, spiky *Edmontonia*, hadrosaurs or "duckbilled" dinosaurs with strange head crests, and of course *T–Rex*.

KEY
1 *Tyrannosaurus rex*
2 *Triceratops*
3 *Stegoceras*
4 *Edmontonia*
5 *Parasaurolophus*
6 *Lambeosaurus*
7 *Avimimus*
8 *Corythosaurus*
9 *Struthiomimus*
10 *Albertosaurus*
11 *Therizinosaurus*
12 *Euoplocephalus*

175 *T–Rex's* full name is *Tyrannosaurus rex*, which means "king of the tyrant lizards." But it wasn't a lizard. It was a large carnivorous or meat-eating animal in the reptile group known as the dinosaurs.

176 Dinosaurs, or "terrible lizards," lived during a time called the Mesozoic Era (252–66 million years ago). The first dinosaurs appeared about 230 million years ago and all had died out, or become extinct, by 66 million years ago.

T-REX

177 There were hundreds of kinds of dinosaurs. *Plateosaurus* was a bus-sized herbivore (plant-eater) from 215 million years ago. *Brachiosaurus* was a giant herbivore from 150 million years ago. *Deinonychus* was a fierce hunter from about 110 million years ago, and was about the size of an adult human.

QUIZ
Which of these extinct animals were dinosaurs?
Pterodactyl
Tyrannosaurus rex
Woolly mammoth
Archaeopteryx   Triceratops
Plateosaurus   Ammonite

Answer:
Tyrannosaurus rex, Triceratops, Plateosaurus

178 *T-Rex* lived well after all of these dinosaurs. Its time was the last part of the Mesozoic Era, known as the Cretaceous Period (145–66 million years ago), from about 68–66 million years ago. *T-Rex* was one of the very last dinosaurs.

ERA	PERIOD	MYA (Million years ago)
MESOZOIC	CRETACEOUS 145.5–65.5 MYA	70, 80, 90, 100, 110, 120, 130, 140
MESOZOIC	JURASSIC 200–145.5 MYA	150, 160, 170, 180, 190
MESOZOIC	TRIASSIC 251–200 MYA	200, 210, 220, 230, 240, 250

Jurassic Period: *Allosaurus* was a big meat-eating dinosaur.

Triassic Period: *Herrerasaurus* was one of the first dinosaurs.

◀ Dinosaurs ruled the land for 185 million years—longer than any other animal group.

A giant predator

179 The size of big, fierce animals such as great white sharks, tigers, and crocodiles can be exaggerated (made bigger). People often think T-Rex was bigger than it really was.

180 A full-grown T-Rex was over 40 feet long and more than 10 feet high at the hips. It could rear up and raise its head to more than 16 feet above the ground.

181 Tyrannosaurus rex was not such a giant compared to some plant-eating animals. It was about the same weight as today's African bush elephant, half the size of the extinct imperial mammoth, and one tenth as heavy as some of the biggest plant-eating dinosaurs.

Brachiosaurus
42 feet tall
82 feet nose to tail
40-plus tons in weight

▼ *Tyrannosaurus rex* may have been big, but it was smaller than all the other creatures shown here.

T-Rex
10–13 feet tall
36–40 feet nose to tail
5.5 tons in weight

Imperial mammoth
14 feet tall
40 feet nose to tail
11 tons in weight

Sperm whale
65 feet nose to tail
55 tons in weight

T-REX

182 Compared to today's biggest meat-eating land animals, *Tyrannosaurus rex* was huge. The largest land carnivores today are polar and grizzly bears, up to 10 feet tall and over 1,300 pounds. However that's only one tenth of the weight of *T-Rex*.

183 Compared to other extinct meat-eaters, *Tyrannosaurus rex* was large. The wolflike *Andrewsarchus* from 40 million years ago was one of the biggest mammal land carnivores. It stood 6.5 feet tall, was 13 feet long from nose to tail, and weighed more than one ton.

184 *Tyrannosaurus rex* is sometimes called "the biggest predator of all time." But it was only one tenth the size of the sperm whale living in today's oceans, which hunts giant squid. It was also smaller than prehistoric ocean predators such as the pliosaurs *Liopleurodon* and *Kronosaurus* (11 tons or more) and the ichthyosaur *Shonisaurus* (more than 22 tons).

COMPARE HUGE HUNTERS

You will need:
pens   large sheet of paper   animal books

In books or on the Internet, find side-on pictures of *T-Rex*, a sperm whale, a killer whale, and *Andrewsarchus*. Draw them on one sheet of paper to see how they compare:
Sperm whale as long as the paper
T-Rex nose to tail two thirds as long as the sperm whale
Killer whale half as long as the sperm whale
Andrewsarchus one fifth as long as the sperm whale

Profile of T-Rex

185 Fossil experts can work out what an extinct animal such as *Tyrannosaurus rex* looked like when it was alive. They study the size, shape, length, thickness, and other details of its fossil bones, teeth, claws, and other parts.

186 The tail of *T-Rex* was almost half its total length. It had a wide, muscular base and was thick and strong almost to the tip, quite unlike the long, thin, whiplike tails of other dinosaurs such as *Diplodocus*.

Backbones (vertebrae) were large, especially at the base of the tail.

Massive muscles could bend the tail base with great power, perhaps to swipe at enemies.

▼ Dinosaurs are divided into two groups, ornithischians (bird-hipped) and saurischians (lizard-hipped). Meat-eaters, including *T rex*, were lizard-hipped. Bird-hipped dinosaurs were plant-eaters.

In lizard-hipped dinosaurs, the lower front part of the hip bone angled down and forward.

In bird-hipped dinosaurs, the lower front part of the hip bone angled down and rearward.

Long foot bones meant that the ankle bones were part way up the leg.

I DON'T BELIEVE IT!
Tyrannosaurus rex's tail was not very bendy or flexible—it stuck out straight behind the body. This is why its group of dinosaurs is called tetanurans or "stiff-tails."

T-REX

187 The fossil bones of T-Rex show that it was a large, heavily built, powerful dinosaur. It had a huge skull, so its head and mouth were massive. There were holes in the skull for the eyes, ears, and nasal openings or nostrils. There were also smaller holes in the bones for blood vessels and nerves.

▼ A cutaway T-Rex shows the thick, strong bones of its skeleton, which have been found preserved in many different fossil remains.

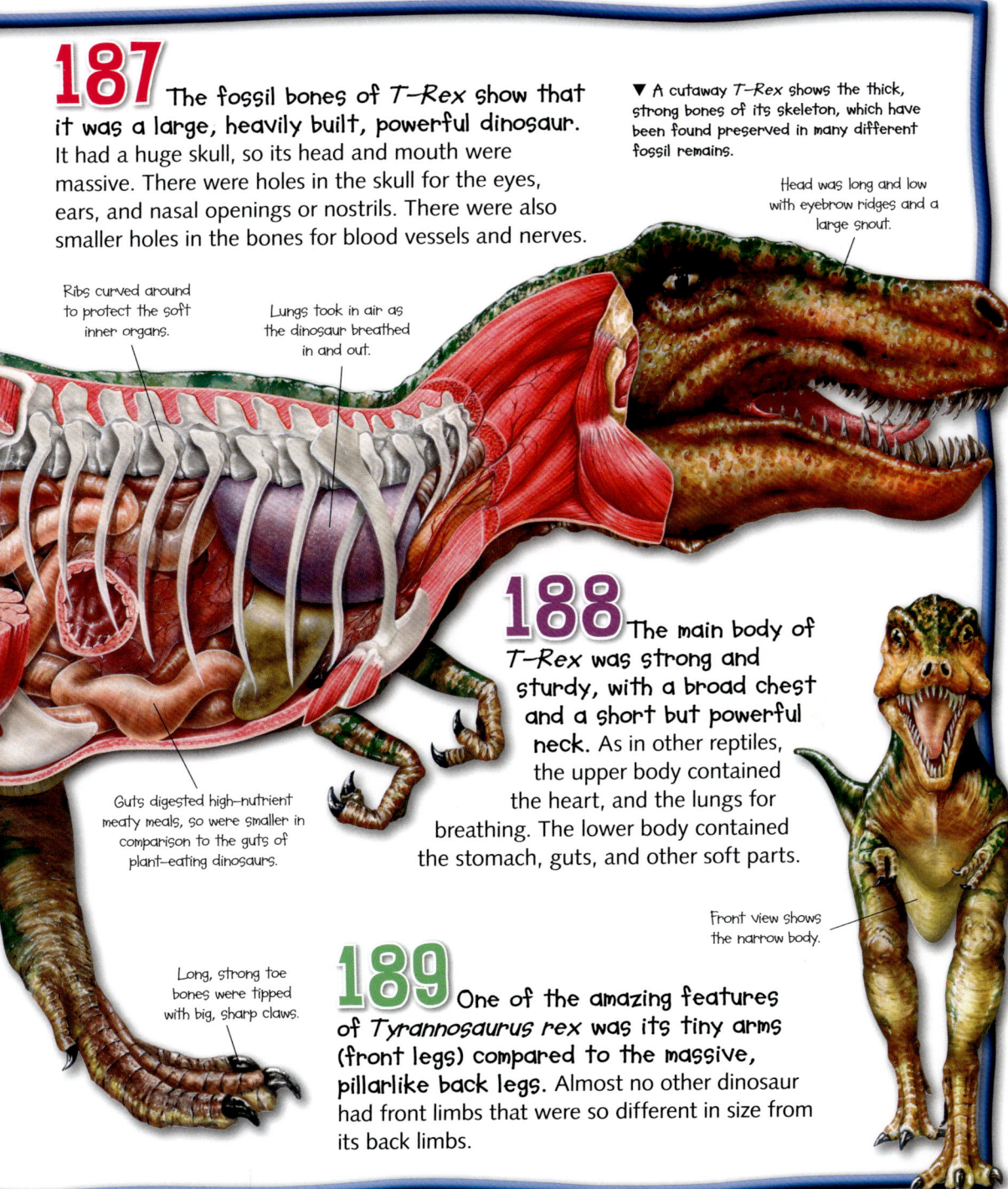

Head was long and low with eyebrow ridges and a large snout.

Ribs curved around to protect the soft inner organs.

Lungs took in air as the dinosaur breathed in and out.

Guts digested high-nutrient meaty meals, so were smaller in comparison to the guts of plant-eating dinosaurs.

188 The main body of T-Rex was strong and sturdy, with a broad chest and a short but powerful neck. As in other reptiles, the upper body contained the heart, and the lungs for breathing. The lower body contained the stomach, guts, and other soft parts.

Front view shows the narrow body.

Long, strong toe bones were tipped with big, sharp claws.

189 One of the amazing features of Tyrannosaurus rex was its tiny arms (front legs) compared to the massive, pillarlike back legs. Almost no other dinosaur had front limbs that were so different in size from its back limbs.

Was T-Rex clever?

▼ Many dinosaurs had eyes on the sides of the head, giving good all-round vision but not a detailed front view. T-Rex had forward-facing eyes.

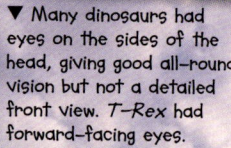

View from forward-facing eyes.

View from sideways-facing eyes.

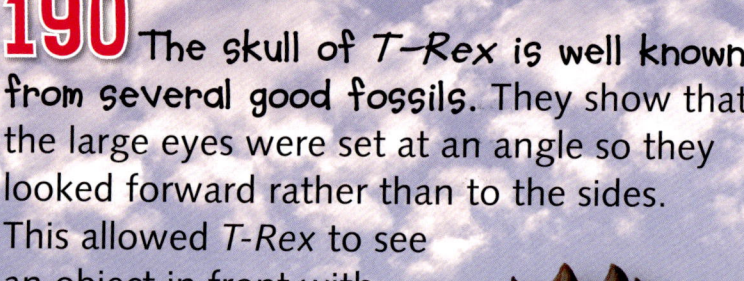

190 The skull of T-Rex is well known from several good fossils. They show that the large eyes were set at an angle so they looked forward rather than to the sides. This allowed T-Rex to see an object in front with both eyes and judge its distance well.

▶ T-Rex probably used its long tongue to lick and taste meat before it started to eat.

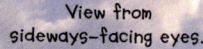

191 As far as we know dinosaurs, like other reptiles, lacked ear flaps. Instead they had eardrums of thin skin on the sides of their heads so they could hear.

T-REX

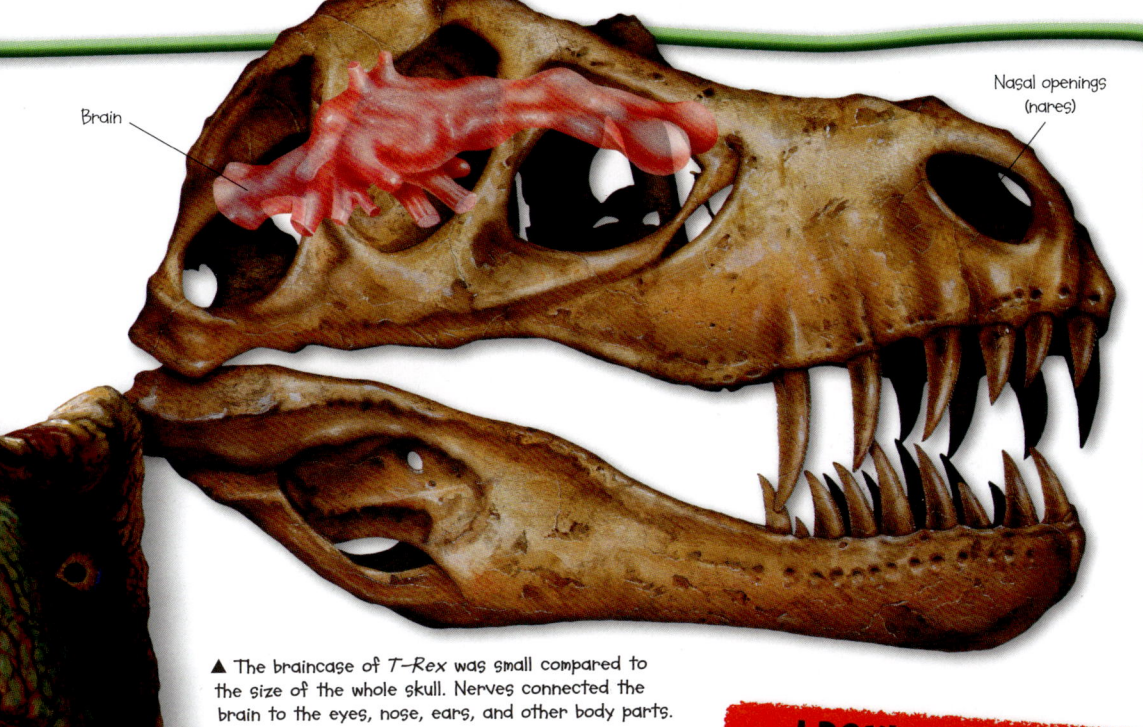

▲ The braincase of T-Rex was small compared to the size of the whole skull. Nerves connected the brain to the eyes, nose, ears, and other body parts.

192 **T-Rex's big nasal openings were at the top of its snout.** They opened into a very large chamber inside the skull, which detected smells floating in the air. T-Rex's sense of smell, like its eyesight, was very good.

I DON'T BELIEVE IT!
The eyeballs of Tyrannosaurus rex were up to 3 inches across—but those of the modern-day giant squid are almost 12 inches!

193 **Some fossils even show the size and shape of T-Rex's brain!** The brain was in a casing called the cranium in the upper rear of the skull. This can be seen in well-preserved skulls. The space inside shows the brain's shape.

194 **Tyrannosaurus rex had the biggest brain of almost any dinosaur.** The parts dealing with the sense of smell, called the olfactory lobes, were especially large. So T-Rex had keen senses of sight, hearing, and especially smell. And it was smart.

What big teeth

195 **Teeth are very hard and make good fossils.** The preserved teeth, jaws, and skulls of T-Rex tell us about the kinds of food it ate.

196 **The skull of a full-grown T-Rex was up to 5 feet long, almost the size of a bathtub.** Like the skulls of other dinosaurs and reptiles, it was made up of more than 20 bones firmly joined together.

197 **T-Rex had 50–60 teeth of different shapes and sizes.** They were up to 12 inches long, but part of this was the root fixed into the jaw. Teeth were bigger in the upper jaw than the lower. They were also slightly smaller and sharper at the front of the mouth. The back teeth were not especially sharp, and are nicknamed "deadly big bananas."

▼ Most of the roughened part of each T-Rex tooth was fixed into the jawbone, with only the smooth part showing.

198 *T–Rex grew new teeth regularly to replace those that wore away or broke off.* This happened in different parts of the mouth at different times. So each T–Rex had a mixture of big older teeth and smaller newer teeth.

199 *The jaw joints of Tyrannosaurus rex were right at the back of its skull.* This allowed the dinosaur to open its jaws wide to take a massive mouthful of food—or perhaps to bite a chunk from a much larger victim.

◀ T–Rex would have used its front teeth to pierce and grip prey. Its side teeth tore flesh, while its back teeth crushed bones and chewed chunks of meat.

▶ Because of its huge teeth and jaw muscles, T–Rex probably had a stronger bite than these living animals.

T-Rex

Alligator

Hyena

Snapping turtle

Great white shark

200 *Scientists' experiments and calculations have compared the bite strength of T–Rex with other creatures alive today.* In bite force units, *Tyrannosaurus rex* usually comes out top!

T-Rex 3,100 (estimated)
Alligator 2,200
Hyena 1,050
Snapping turtle 1,000
Lion 950

Great white shark 650
Wolf 400
Hyacinth macaw 355
Labrador dog 150
Human 120

Tiny arms, big legs

201 *Tyrannosaurus rex's strangest features were its tiny arms.* In fact, they were about the same size as the arms of an adult human, even though *T-Rex* was more than 50 times bigger than a person. Yet the arms were not weak. They had powerful muscles and two strong clawed fingers.

▶ T-Rex's arms were so small, they could not even be used for passing food to the mouth.

202 *What did Tyrannosaurus rex use its mini-arms for?* There have been many suggestions such as holding onto a victim while biting, pushing itself off the ground if it fell over, and holding onto a partner at breeding time. Perhaps we will never know the true reason.

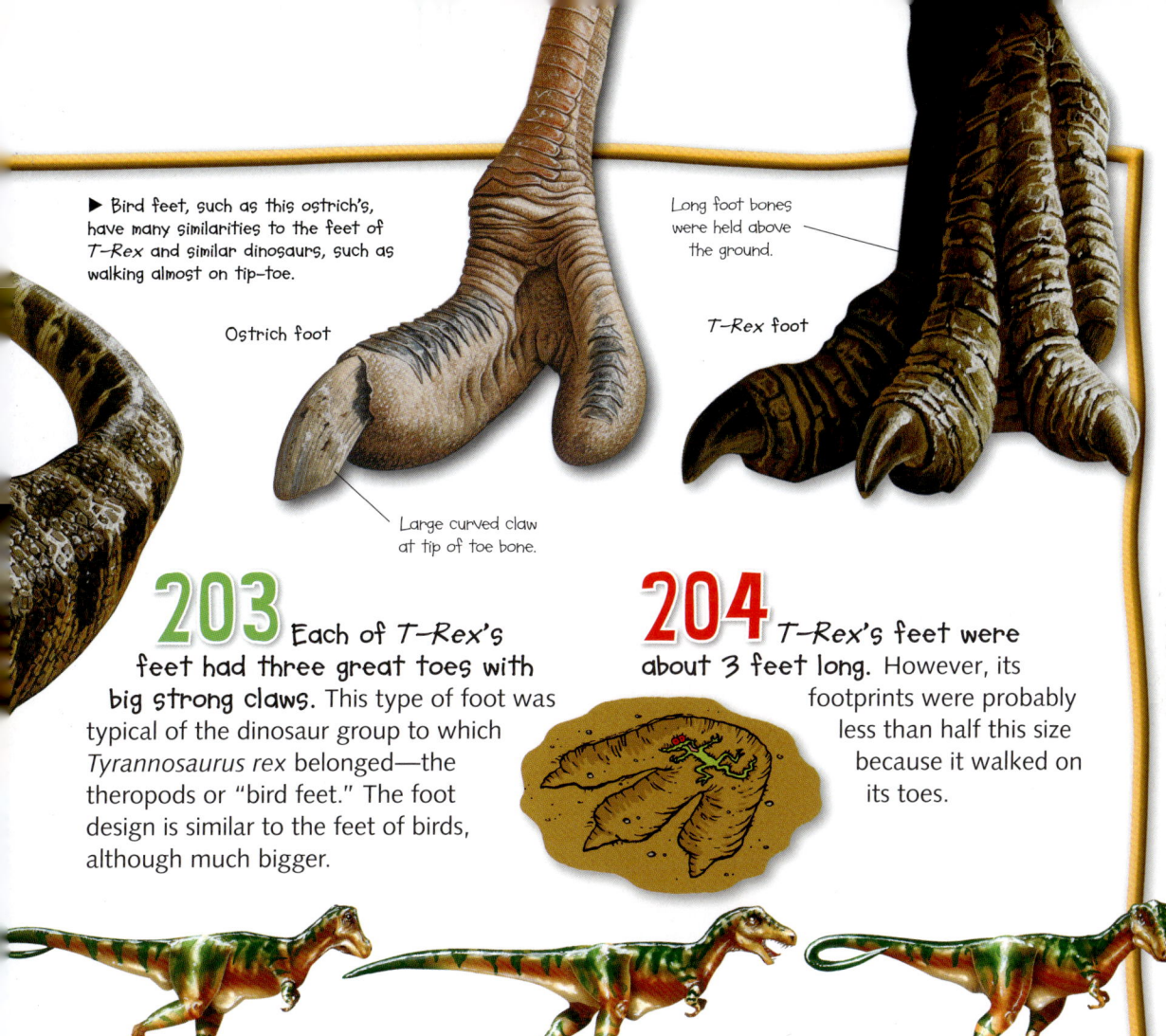

▶ Bird feet, such as this ostrich's, have many similarities to the feet of T-Rex and similar dinosaurs, such as walking almost on tip-toe.

Ostrich foot

Long foot bones were held above the ground.

T-Rex foot

Large curved claw at tip of toe bone.

203 Each of T-Rex's feet had three great toes with big strong claws. This type of foot was typical of the dinosaur group to which Tyrannosaurus rex belonged—the theropods or "bird feet." The foot design is similar to the feet of birds, although much bigger.

204 T-Rex's feet were about 3 feet long. However, its footprints were probably less than half this size because it walked on its toes.

▲ As T-Rex ran it probably kept its head, neck, main body, and tail in a line, almost horizontal or level with the ground.

205 The big, heavy back legs of Tyrannosaurus rex show that the dinosaur could make long strides as it walked and ran. The three parts of the leg—the thigh, shin, and foot—were all about the same length.

206 Trackways are fossil footprints in mud and sand that give clues to how an animal moved. There are some trackways that could have been made by Tyrannosaurus rex or similar dinosaurs. They help to show how fast it walked and ran.

What did *T-Rex* eat?

207 *Tyrannosaurus rex* was a huge hunter, so it probably ate big prey. Other large dinosaurs of its time and place were plant-eaters. They included three-horned *Triceratops* and its cousins, and various "duck-billed" dinosaurs (hadrosaurs) such as *Parasaurolophus* and *Edmontosaurus*.

▼ The giant pterosaur (flying reptile) *Quetzalcoatlus* lived at about the same time as *T-Rex*. It may have pecked at the remains of a *T-Rex* kill after the dinosaur had finished feasting.

208 *T-Rex* could have used its huge mouth, strong teeth, and powerful jaw muscles to attack big plant-eaters. It may have lunged at a victim with one massive bite to cause a slashing wound. Then it would retreat a short distance and wait for the prey to weaken from blood loss before moving in to feed.

◀ An adult *Triceratops* would be a fierce foe for *T-Rex* to tackle. However young, sick, and old *Triceratops* might have been easier to kill.

209 One fossil of *Triceratops* has scratchlike gouge marks on its large, bony neck frill. These could have been made by *Tyrannosaurus rex* teeth. The marks are about the correct distance apart, matching the spacing of *T-Rex* teeth.

▶ The hadrosaur *Parasaurolophus* might have made loud trumpeting noises through its hollow tubelike head crest, to warn others in its herd that *T-Rex* was near.

T-REX

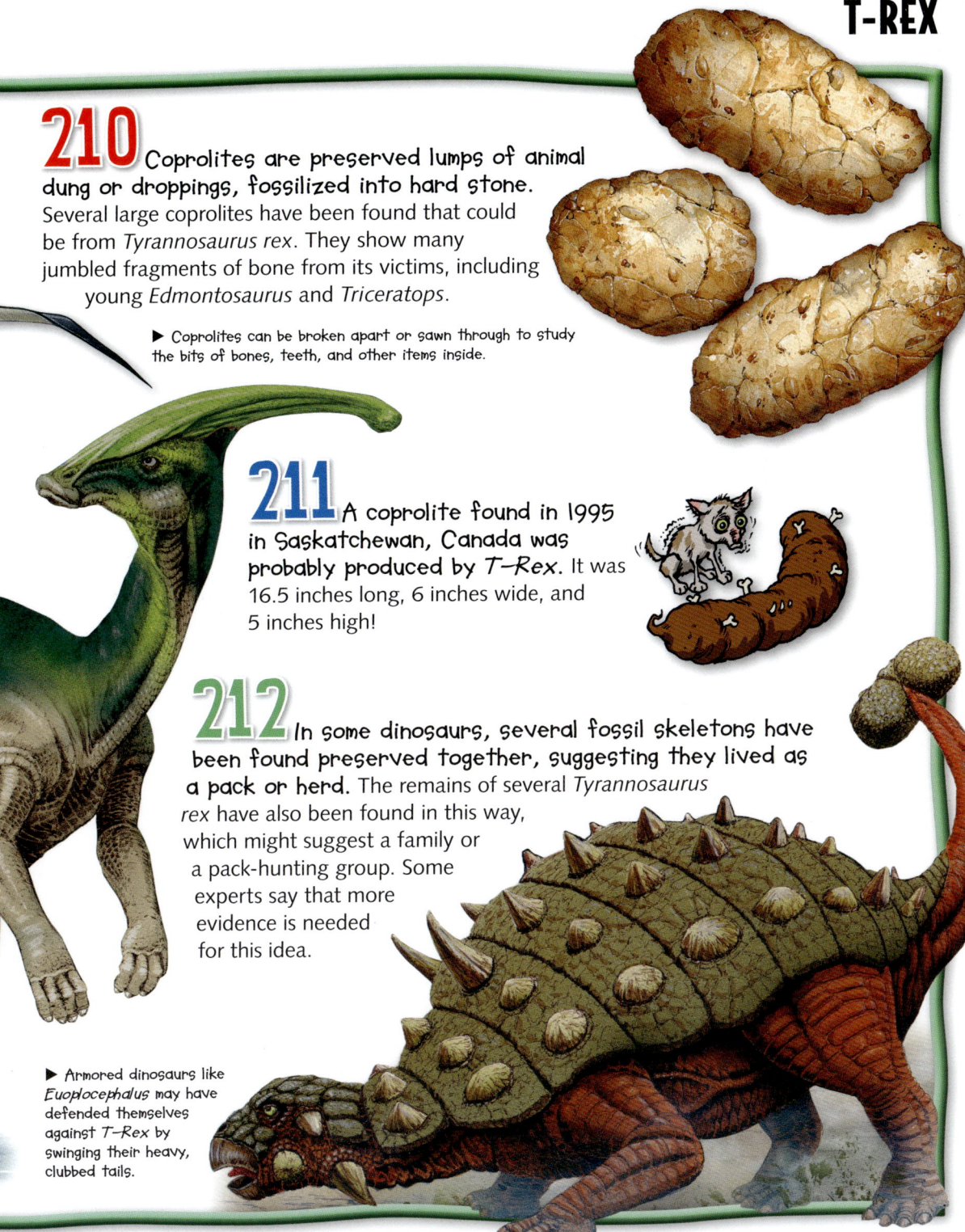

210 Coprolites are preserved lumps of animal dung or droppings, fossilized into hard stone. Several large coprolites have been found that could be from *Tyrannosaurus rex*. They show many jumbled fragments of bone from its victims, including young *Edmontosaurus* and *Triceratops*.

▶ Coprolites can be broken apart or sawn through to study the bits of bones, teeth, and other items inside.

211 A coprolite found in 1995 in Saskatchewan, Canada was probably produced by *T-Rex*. It was 16.5 inches long, 6 inches wide, and 5 inches high!

212 In some dinosaurs, several fossil skeletons have been found preserved together, suggesting they lived as a pack or herd. The remains of several *Tyrannosaurus rex* have also been found in this way, which might suggest a family or a pack-hunting group. Some experts say that more evidence is needed for this idea.

▶ Armored dinosaurs like *Euoplocephalus* may have defended themselves against *T-Rex* by swinging their heavy, clubbed tails.

Hunter or scavenger?

213 Was *T-Rex* an active hunter that chased after its victims? Was it an ambush predator that hid in wait to rush out at prey? Was it a scavenger that ate any dead or dying dinosaurs it found? Or did it chase other dinosaurs from their kills and steal the meal for itself?

214 To be an active pursuit hunter, *T-Rex* must have been able to run fast. Scientists have tried to work out its running speed using models and computers, and by comparisons with other animals.

WHO DOES WHAT?
Research these animals living today and find out if they are mainly fast hunters, sneaky ambushers, or scavengers.
Tiger Cheetah Hyena
Crocodile Vulture
African wild dog

▶ *Tyrannosaurus rex* may have run down smaller dinosaurs such as these *Prenocephale*, perhaps rushing out from its hiding place in a clump of trees.

T-REX

▲ When scavenging, T-Rex might sniff out a dinosaur that had died from illness or injury.

▲ When hunting, T-Rex would be at risk from injury, such as from the horns of Triceratops.

215 Some estimates for the running speed of T-Rex are as fast as 30 miles an hour, others as slow as 9 miles an hour. Most give a speed of between 12 and 18 miles an hour. This is slightly slower than a human sprinter, but probably faster than typical T-Rex prey such as Triceratops.

216 Several T-Rex fossils show injuries to body parts such as shins, ribs, neck, and jaws. These could have been made by victims fighting back, suggesting that T-Rex hunted live prey.

▶ T-Rex would tear and rip flesh from large prey, gulp in lumps, and swallow them whole.

217 Evidence that T-Rex was a scavenger includes its very well developed sense of smell for sniffing out dead, rotting bodies. Also, its powerful teeth could not chew food repeatedly like we do, but they could crush bones at first bite to get at the nutritious jellolike marrow inside. Maybe a hungry Tyrannosaurus rex simply ate anything it could catch or find, so it was a hunter, ambusher, and scavenger all in one.

Growing up

218 **Did T-Rex live in groups?** Most of its fossils are of lone individuals. Some were found near other specimens of T-Rex. These could have been preserved near each other by chance, or they could have been a group that all died together.

Embryo Yolk

▲ A baby dinosaur developed as an embryo in its egg, fed by nutrients from the yolk.

▶ The baby probably hatched out by biting through the tough shell, which was flexible like leather.

219 **Living reptiles lay eggs that hatch into young, and dinosaurs such as T-Rex probably did the same.** Many fossil dinosaur eggs have been discovered, but none are known for certain to be from T-Rex. Some dinosaurs laid eggs in nests and looked after their young, but again there are no fossils like this for T-Rex.

221 **It seems that T-Rex grew slowly for about 12–14 years.** Then suddenly it grew very fast, putting on about 4 pounds every day as a teenager. By 20 years it was full-grown.

▶ Young T-Rex may have killed small prey such as birds, lizards, and newly hatched dinosaurs.

220 **Fossils of individual T-Rex are of different sizes and ages, showing how this dinosaur grew up.** Some of the fossil bones are so well preserved that they have "growth rings" almost like a tree trunk, showing growth speed.

T-REX

222 **Can we tell apart female and male *Tyrannosaurus rex* from their fossils?** Some scientists thought that females were bigger, with stronger, thicker bones than the males. However the latest evidence makes this less clear.

▶ In many reptiles today, the adults keep growing with age. However their growth rate gradually reduces, so they get bigger more slowly. It is not certain if dinosaurs such as T-Rex grew like this.

223 **The biggest T-Rex found, "Sue," was about 28 years old when it died.** No one knows for certain if *Tyrannosaurus rex* could live longer. As with many of these questions, more fossil finds will help to fill in the details.

Where in the world?

224 T-Rex was one kind, or species, of dinosaur in a group of species known as the genus *Tyrannosaurus*. Were there any other members of this genus?

225 After T-Rex fossils were discovered and named over 100 years ago, fossil-hunters began to find the remains of similar huge predators. Some were given their own names in the genus *Tyrannosaurus*, but most have now been renamed *Tyrannosaurus rex*.

226 *Tarbosaurus*, "terrifying lizard," was very similar to T-Rex, almost as big, and it lived at the same time. However its fossils come from Asia—Mongolia and China—rather than North America. Some experts consider it to be another species of *Tyrannosaurus*, called *Tyrannosaurus bataar*. Others think that it's so similar to T-Rex that it should be called *Tyrannosaurus rex*.

227 Fossils of smaller dinosaurs similar to T-Rex have been found in Europe. They include the 20-foot-long *Eotyrannus*, from more than 100 million years ago, from the Isle of Wight, southern England. Fossils of *Aviatyrannis* from Portugal are even older, and date from the Jurassic Period.

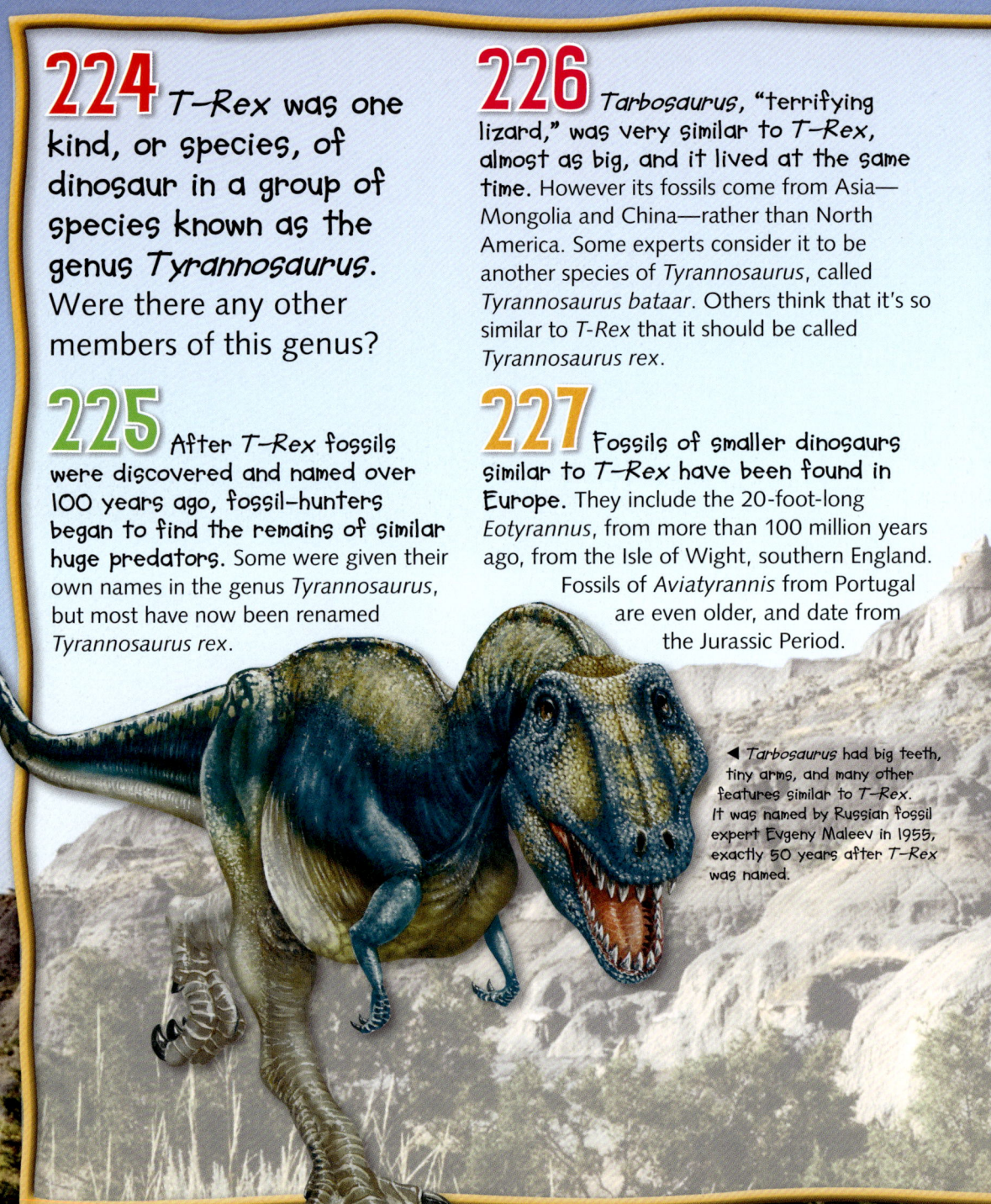

◄ *Tarbosaurus* had big teeth, tiny arms, and many other features similar to T-Rex. It was named by Russian fossil expert Evgeny Maleev in 1955, exactly 50 years after T-Rex was named.

T-REX

228 In 1979, the remains of a big Asian meat-eating dinosaur in the same genus as *Tyrannosaurus rex* were named as *Tyrannosaurus luanchuanensis*. After much discussion another name, *Jenghizkhan*, was suggested. However some scientists say that like *Tarbosaurus*, *Jenghizkhan* is so similar to *T-Rex* that it should be called *Tyrannosaurus*.

229 A fossil skull found in 1942 was named *Nanotyrannus*, "tiny tyrant." It may be a separate kind of small tyrannosaur—or simply a young *T-Rex*. Experts are undecided.

▼ Many *T-Rex* fossils come from rock layers known as the Hell Creek Formation. These are found mainly in Montana.

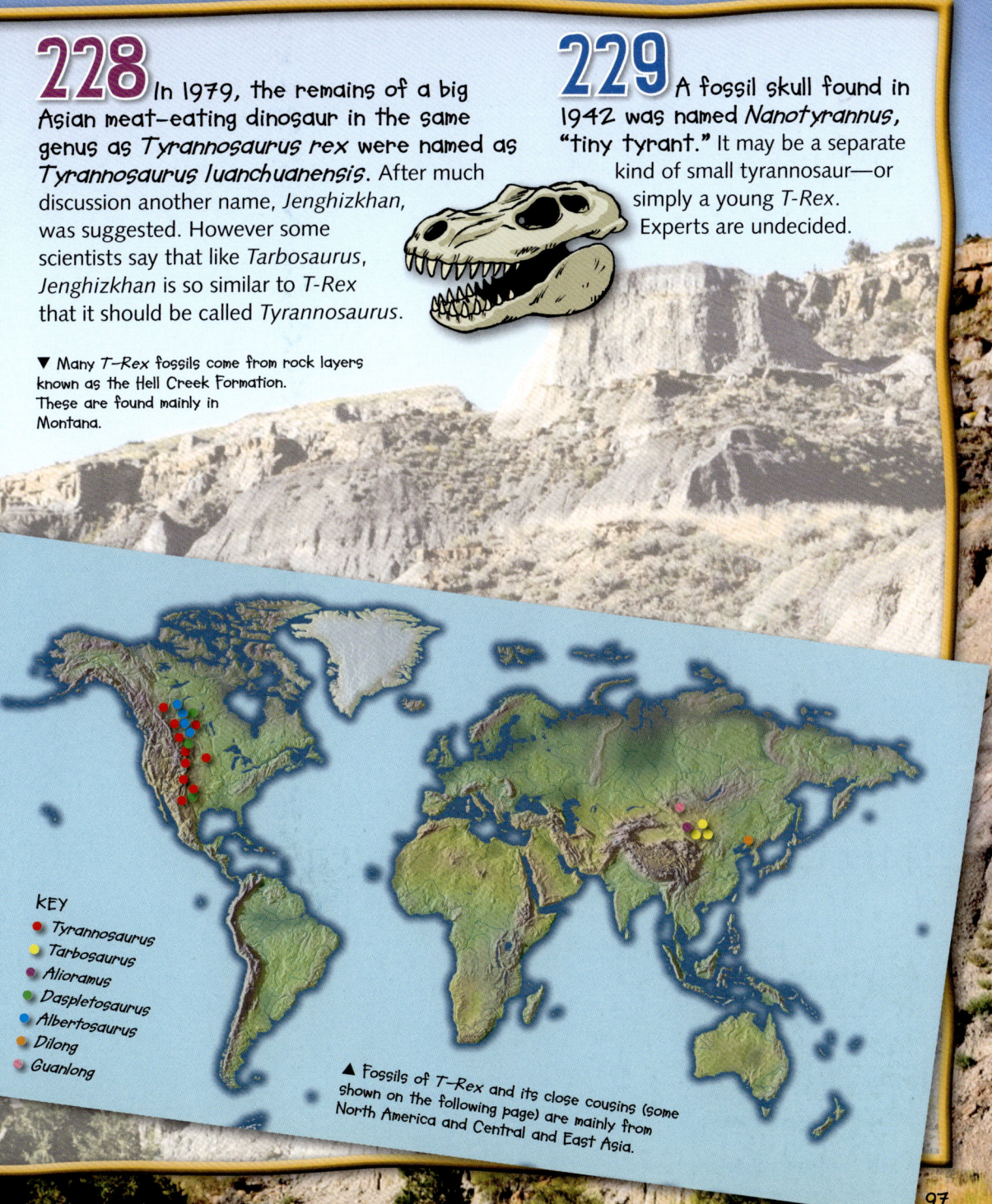

KEY
- Tyrannosaurus
- Tarbosaurus
- Alioramus
- Daspletosaurus
- Albertosaurus
- Dilong
- Guanlong

▲ Fossils of *T-Rex* and its close cousins (some shown on the following page) are mainly from North America and Central and East Asia.

Tyrannosaur group

230 **What kind of dinosaur was *Tyrannosaurus rex*?** It belonged to the group called tyrannosaurs, known scientifically as the family *Tyrannosauridae*. These dinosaurs had bones, joints, and other features that were different from other predatory dinosaurs. They were part of an even bigger group, the tyrannosauroids.

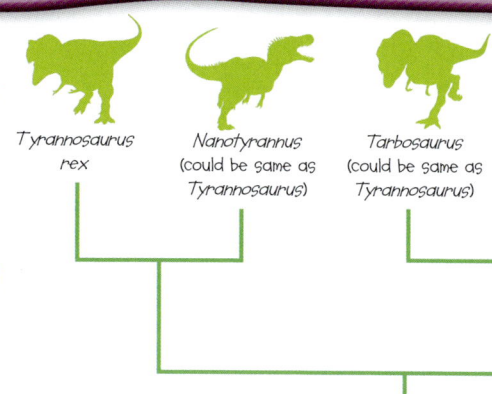

231 One of the first tyrannosauroids was *Guanlong*, "crown dragon." Its fossils were discovered in China in 2006 and are about 160 million years old—nearly 100 million years before *Tyrannosaurus rex*. It was 10 feet long and had a strange hornlike plate of bone on its nose.

▲ *Guanlong* may have shown off the crest of thin bone on its head to possible partners at breeding time.

▼ The "feathers" of *Dilong* were similar to fur and may have kept its body warm.

232 Another early cousin of T-Rex was *Dilong*, "emperor dragon," also from China. Its fossils date to 130 million years ago. *Dilong* was about 6.5 feet long when fully grown. It had traces of hairlike feathers on the head and tail. As shown later, some experts suggest *Tyrannosaurus rex* itself may have had some kind of feathers.

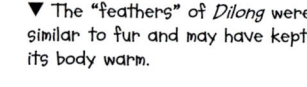

T-REX

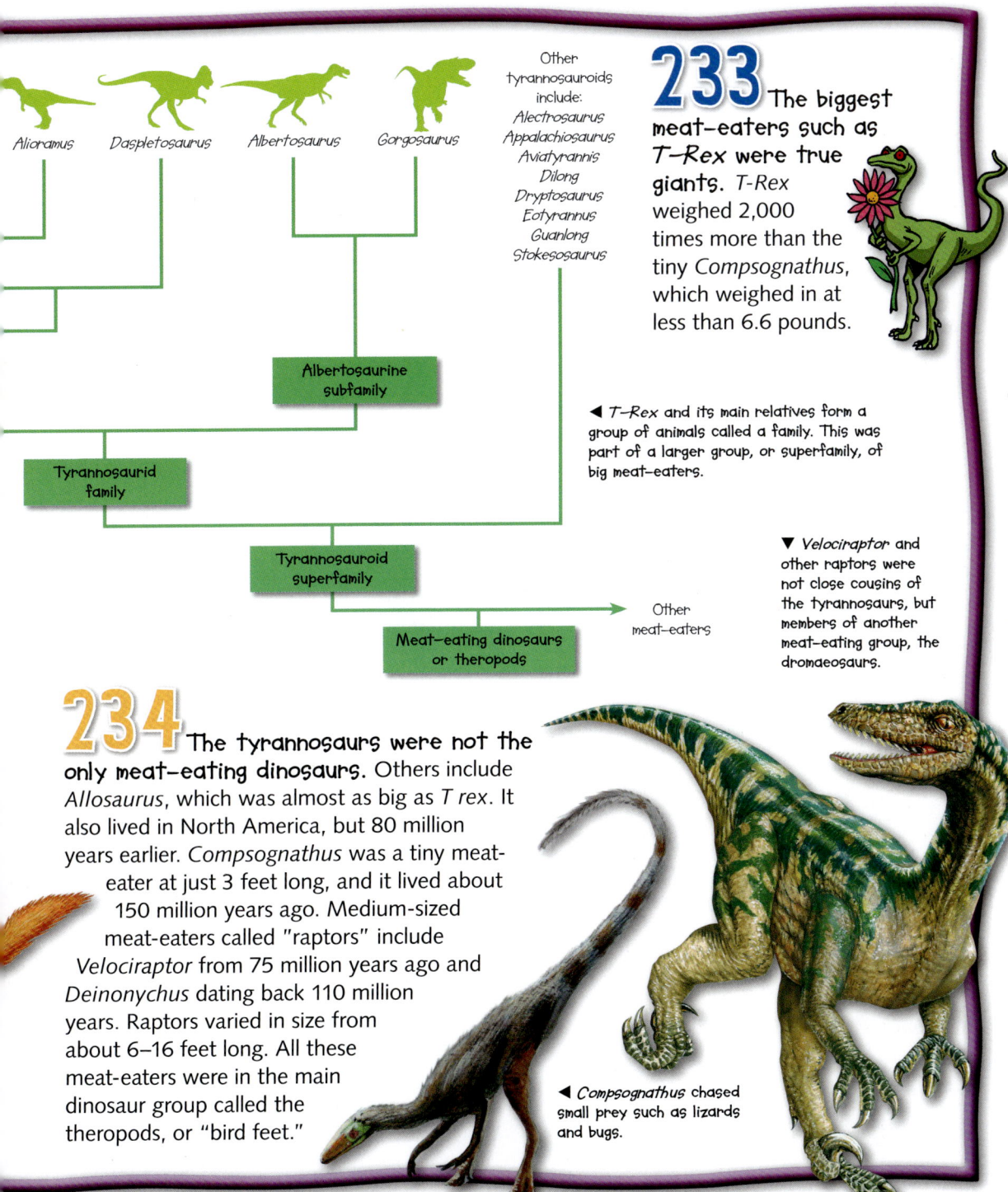

Other tyrannosauroids include:
Alectrosaurus
Appalachiosaurus
Aviatyrannis
Dilong
Dryptosaurus
Eotyrannus
Guanlong
Stokesosaurus

233 The biggest meat-eaters such as *T-Rex* were true giants. T-Rex weighed 2,000 times more than the tiny *Compsognathus*, which weighed in at less than 6.6 pounds.

◀ *T-Rex* and its main relatives form a group of animals called a family. This was part of a larger group, or superfamily, of big meat-eaters.

▼ *Velociraptor* and other raptors were not close cousins of the tyrannosaurs, but members of another meat-eating group, the dromaeosaurs.

234 The tyrannosaurs were not the only meat-eating dinosaurs. Others include *Allosaurus*, which was almost as big as *T rex*. It also lived in North America, but 80 million years earlier. *Compsognathus* was a tiny meat-eater at just 3 feet long, and it lived about 150 million years ago. Medium-sized meat-eaters called "raptors" include *Velociraptor* from 75 million years ago and *Deinonychus* dating back 110 million years. Raptors varied in size from about 6–16 feet long. All these meat-eaters were in the main dinosaur group called the theropods, or "bird feet."

◀ *Compsognathus* chased small prey such as lizards and bugs.

Close cousins

235 In the tyrannosaur group with *T-Rex* were several of its closest relatives. They were big, fierce dinosaurs, but most lived before *T-Rex* and were not quite as large.

236 *Albertosaurus* is named after a princess. Its fossils come from the Canadian province Alberta, which was named in honor of Louise Caroline Alberta, daughter of Britain's Queen Victoria and Prince Albert.

▲ There are many fossil remains of *Gorgosaurus*, making it one of the best known of all the tyrannosaurs. It had a small hornlike crest above each eye.

237 Fossils of *Gorgosaurus*, "fierce lizard," come mainly from Alberta, Canada and are 75–70 million years old. *Gorgosaurus* was very similar to *Albertosaurus*, although slightly smaller at 26–29 feet long. Like all tyrannosaurs, it had hollow bones and openings in its skull that helped to reduce its weight. Some experts think that *Gorgosaurus* was really a kind of *Albertosaurus* and that its name should be changed.

T-REX

238 *Daspletosaurus*, "frightful lizard," was another dinosaur from Alberta, 80–75 million years ago. Its fossils are also known from other regions of North America, as far south as New Mexico. It was about 26 feet long with especially large jaws and teeth. Its arms were small, but not quite so tiny compared to its body as those of *Tyrannosaurus rex*.

▲ *Daspletosaurus* weighed about 2.5 tons and had a skull more than 3 feet long.

▼ *Alectrosaurus* from Mongolia, Asia was one of the smaller tyrannosaurs, at 16 feet in length.

▶ *Appalachiosaurus* fossils come from Alabama, which is an area where few other tyrannosaurs have been found. Only one 23-foot-long skeleton has been found, but it was probably not fully grown.

239 *Albertosaurus*, "Alberta lizard," dates from about 75–70 million years ago. Its fossils were first found in Alberta, Canada. It looked similar to *T-Rex*, with a huge mouth and sharp teeth, small arms, and powerful legs, but it was smaller, at 29–32 feet and around 1.5 tons. At one site the remains of over 20 *Albertosaurus* were found, from adults to teenagers to youngsters. This could have been a mixed pack out hunting.

Discovering T-Rex

240 The first fossils of T-Rex were found in the 1870s by Arthur Lakes and John Bell Hatcher, in Wyoming. However these were not recognized as T-Rex until years later. In 1892, fossil expert Edward Drinker Cope found remains of a big meat-eater and named them *Manospondylus*. Over 100 years later these remains were restudied and renamed as T-Rex.

▲ Edward Drinker Cope (1840–97) named many other kinds of dinosaurs in addition to T-Rex, including *Camarasaurus*, *Amphicoelias*, *Coelophysis*, *Hadrosaurus*, and *Monoclonius*.

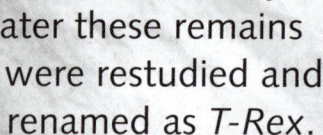

▶ The fossil bones of big dinosaurs such as T–Rex are solid stone and very heavy. Many years ago, horses dragged them from rocky, remote areas to the nearest road or railway.

241 In 1900, again in Wyoming, leading fossil collector Barnum Brown found the first partial skeleton of *Tyrannosaurus rex*, rather than scattered single bones and teeth. At first the fossils were named as *Dynamosaurus* by Henry Fairfield Osborn of the American Museum of Natural History in New York.

T-REX

I DON'T BELIEVE IT!
Osborn's report of 1905 included several kinds of dinosaurs. Due to a mix-up with the names, T-Rex was almost called *Dynamosaurus imperiosus*. So T-Rex could have been D-Imp!

242 *T-Rex* fossils have always been greatly prized by museums, exhibitions, and private collectors. In 1941, the fossils that Brown found in 1902 were sold to the Carnegie Museum of Natural History in Pittsburgh, Pennsylvania, for a huge sum of money. Searching for, selling, and buying *T-Rex* fossils continues today.

▼ Barnum Brown was the most famous fossil-hunter of his time. He sometimes wore a thick fur coat—even when digging for fossils in the scorching sun.

243 Barnum Brown discovered parts of another *Tyrannosaurus rex* fossil skeleton at Hell Creek, Montana, in 1902. In 1905, Osborn wrote a scientific description of these remains and called them *Tyrannosaurus rex*. This was the first time the official name was used. In a way, it was when T-Rex was "born."

BARNUM BROWN—DINOSAUR DETECTIVE
Barnum Brown (1873–1963) collected not only dinosaur fossils, but fossils of all kinds, and other scientific treasures such as crystals. He and his teams worked for the American Museum of Natural History in New York. They traveled to remote places, and if there were rivers but no roads, they used a large raft as a floating base camp. They worked fast too, often blasting apart rocks with dynamite. Brown also made a living by informing oil companies about the best places to drill for oil.

244 In 1906, Brown found an even better part-skeleton of *Tyrannosaurus rex* in Montana. The same year, Osborn realized that the *Dynamosaurus* fossils were extremely similar to *Tyrannosaurus rex*, so he renamed those too as *Tyrannosaurus rex*. The public began to hear about this huge, fierce, meat-eating monster from long ago, and soon its fame was growing fast.

Rebuilding T-Rex

245 Fossil experts use preserved bones and other parts of T-Rex to show what it looked like when alive. The bones are also compared to those of similar animals alive today, known as comparative anatomy. For T-Rex, similar living animals include crocodiles, lizards—and birds.

247 As with other extinct creatures, there are no remains of T-Rex's soft body parts such as the stomach, guts, heart, and lungs. These were eaten by scavengers soon after death or were rotted away. However experts can use comparative anatomy with living creatures to imagine what T-Rex's soft body parts looked like.

▼ Fossil dinosaur skin has a scaly surface, similar to many of today's reptiles.

246 Some fossil bones have patches, grooves, and ridges called "muscle scars." They show where the animal's muscles were joined to the bones in life. This helps experts to work out how the muscles pulled the bones and how T-Rex moved when it was alive.

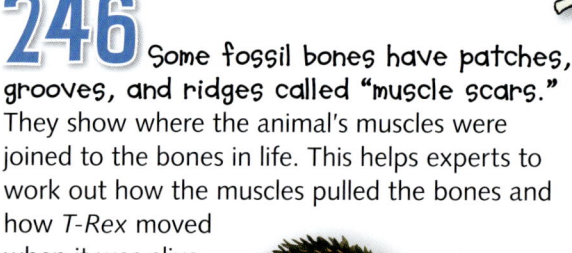

248 Skin and scales of dinosaurs sometimes form fossils. However they are the color of the rocks that make the fossils, not the color of the original skin and scales. So we have no way of knowing T-Rex's true color in life.

◄ Close cousins of T-Rex have been preserved with simple hairlike feathers on their skin. It may be possible that T-Rex also had feathers.

T-REX

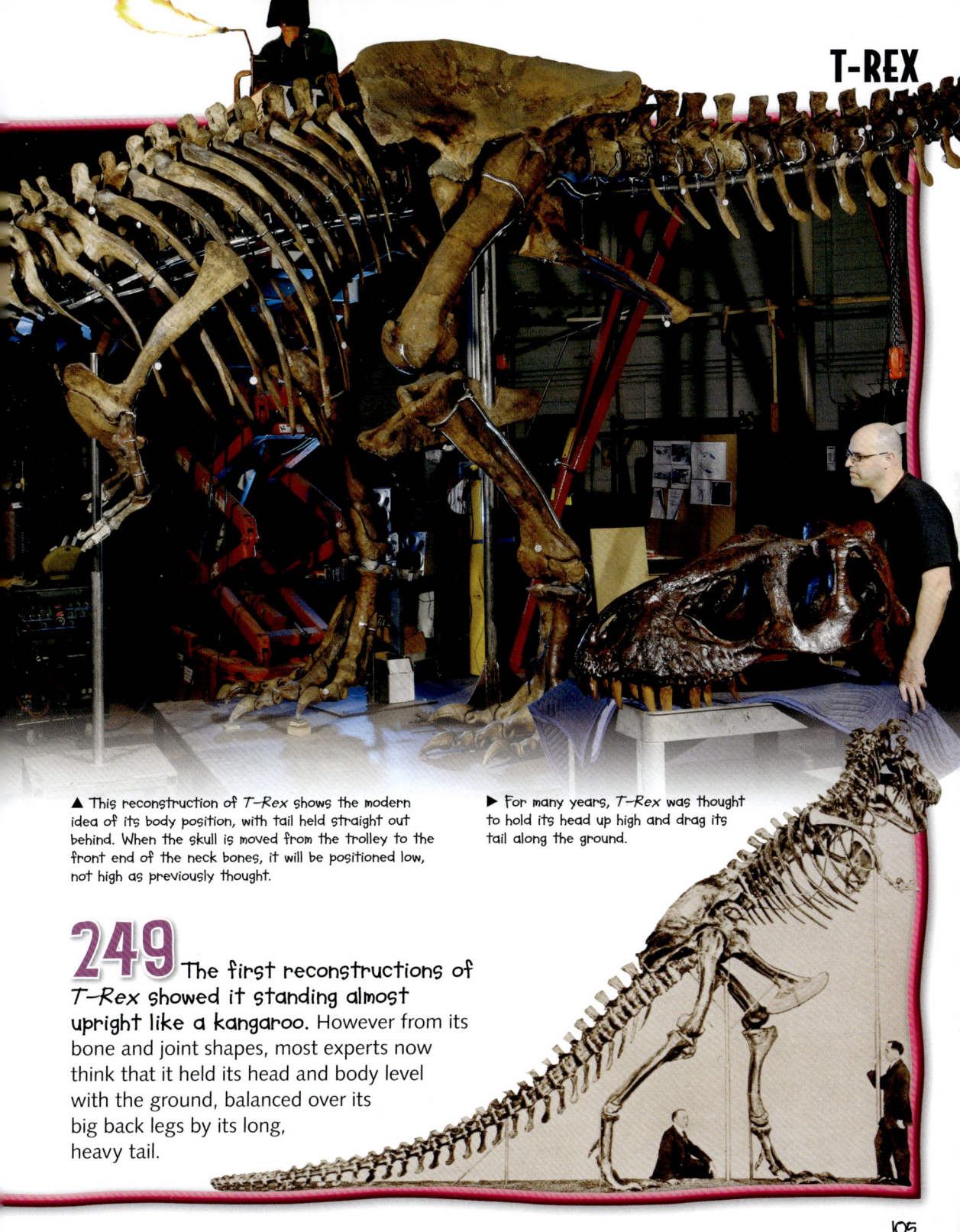

▲ This reconstruction of T-Rex shows the modern idea of its body position, with tail held straight out behind. When the skull is moved from the trolley to the front end of the neck bones, it will be positioned low, not high as previously thought.

▶ For many years, T-Rex was thought to hold its head up high and drag its tail along the ground.

249 The first reconstructions of T-Rex showed it standing almost upright like a kangaroo. However from its bone and joint shapes, most experts now think that it held its head and body level with the ground, balanced over its big back legs by its long, heavy tail.

The story of Sue

250 **The biggest *Tyrannosaurus rex* found so far is called "Sue."** Its official code number is FMNH PR2081, from the Field Museum of Natural History in Chicago where it is stored.

251 **"Sue" is named after its discoverer, Sue Hendrickson.** She was working at a fossil dig in 1990 near the town of Faith, in South Dakota, when she uncovered parts of a massive *T-Rex*. An entire team of people helped to dig up and clean the remains.

252 **With about four fifths of its teeth, bones, and other parts preserved, "Sue" is amazingly complete for a fossil animal.** The dinosaur was probably covered with mud soon after it died, which prevented scavenging animals from cracking open or carrying away its bones.

253 **"Sue" dates from between 67 and 65.5 million years ago.** It measures 42 feet from nose to tail-tip and 13 feet tall at the hips. The weight of "Sue" when alive was probably around 6 tons.

◀ Sue Hendrickson with the fossil foot of "Sue." As well as finding "Sue" the *T-Rex*, Sue Hendrickson is an expert diver and has explored shipwrecks and sunken cities.

▼ In May 2000, "Sue" went on display at the Field Museum of Chicago and has been the star attraction ever since.

I DON'T BELIEVE IT!
Despite the name "Sue," it's not clear if this T-Rex specimen was female or male. But it's a true "Sue-perstar" with more than a million visitors each year!

254 **After "Sue" was discovered, there was a dispute about who owned the fossils.** Various people claimed them, including the landowner, the dig team, the organizers of the excavation, and the local authorities. After a legal battle, "Sue" was sold at auction in 1997 in New York. The Field Museum of Chicago paid $8.39 million.

Stan, Jane, and the rest

255 Apart from "Sue," there are more than 30 other sets of T-Rex fossils. Some are just a few bones and teeth, while others are well preserved, fairly complete skeletons.

256 "Stan" is named after its discoverer Stan Sacrisen. Code numbered BHI 3033, it was dug up near Buffalo, South Dakota in 1992 by a team from the Black Hills Institute. "Stan" was about 40 feet long and 3.3 tons in weight, with 199 bones and 58 teeth. Some bones show signs of injuries that had healed, including broken ribs, a damaged neck, and a tooth wound in the skull.

257 "Wankel rex," specimen MOR 555, was found by Kathy Wankel in 1988. It was excavated by a team from the Museum of the Rockies and is now on show at that museum in Bozeman, Montana.

258 "Tinker," also called "Kid Rex," was a young *Tyrannosaurus rex*. About two thirds adult size, it was found in 1998 in South Dakota and named after the leader of the fossil-hunting team, Ron "Tinker" Frithiof.

▶ "Stan" is now at the Black Hills Museum in Hill City, South Dakota.

T-REX

259 "Jane" is specimen BMRP 2002.4.1 at the Burpee Museum of Natural History, Rockford, Illinois. Found in Montana, it's smaller than a full grown *T-Rex*, at 20 feet long and 1,400–1,500 pounds. Some experts believe it is a part-grown youngster, probably 10–12 years old when it died. Others say it is a similar but smaller kind of dinosaur named *Nanotyrannus*.

▶ The fossils of "Jane" from Montana's Hell Creek took more than four years to dig out, clean up, and put together for display.

NEW NAME FOR *T-REX*

You will need:
pictures of *T-Rex* in different poses
pen   paper

Copy some pictures of *T-Rex* onto your paper. Imagine you and your friends have discovered their fossils and given them nicknames. Write these next to your drawings. Perhaps *T-Rex* should be named after you?

Bigger than the "king"

260 Until the 1990s, *Tyrannosaurus rex* was famous as the biggest predatory land creature of all time. However the past few years have seen discoveries of even bigger meat-eating dinosaurs.

261 Fossils of *Giganotosaurus*, "southern giant reptile," were uncovered in 1993 in Patagonia, Argentina. This huge hunter was slightly bigger than *T-Rex*, at more than 42 feet long and weighing over 6.6 tons. *Giganotosaurus* lived earlier than *T-Rex*, about 95–90 million years ago.

262 Fossils of *Spinosaurus* were first found in Egypt in 1912. This predator lived 100–95 million years ago, and had long, bony rods sticking up from its back that may have held up a "sail" of skin. The first find suggested a big predator, although not as big as *T-Rex*. But recent finds indicate *Spinosaurus* may have been larger, maybe 53 feet long and more than 7 tons in weight.

QUIZ

Put these dinosaurs in order of size, biggest to smallest:

Tyrannosaurus rex Deinonychus Brachiosaurus Spinosaurus Compsognathus Giganotosaurus

Answers:
Brachiosaurus, Spinosaurus, Giganotosaurus, Tyrannosaurus rex, Deinonychus, Compsognathus

T-REX

263 *Carcharodontosaurus*, "shark tooth lizard," was another massive hunter from North Africa. It was first named in 1931 and lived 100–95 million years ago. Recent discoveries in Morocco and Niger show that it could have been about the same size as T-Rex.

264 Another *T-Rex*-sized dinosaur was *Mapusaurus*, which lived in Argentina around the same time as *T-Rex* lived in North America. It was not as heavily built as *T-Rex*, weighing about 3 tons.

▼ This skull of *Carcharodontosaurus* measures more than 5.5 feet in length, with teeth 7 inches long. The human skull just in front of it gives an idea of just how big this dinosaur was.

▶ T-Rex and the other meat-eaters were not the biggest dinosaurs by far. Much larger are huge plant-eaters such as *Brachiosaurus* and *Argentinosaurus*.

T-Rex superstar

265 *Tyrannosaurus rex is far more than a big meat-eating dinosaur.* It's a world superstar, alongside such famous creatures as the great white shark, blue whale, gorilla, tiger, and golden eagle. If *Tyrannosaurus rex* was alive today and could charge money for using its name, pictures, sponsorships, and advertising, it would be mega-rich!

266 *T-Rex was one of the stars of the Jurassic Park movies.* However it didn't live in the Jurassic Period, it lived 80 million years later at the end of the Cretaceous Period.

267 *Ever since its fossils were discovered, T-Rex has starred in books, plays, and movies.* It's featured in films such as *The Lost World* (first made in 1925, then again in 1960 and 1992), several *King Kong* movies, the animated *The Land Before Time* (1988), and the *Night at the Museum* movies (2006, 2009, and 2014).

▼ In *Night at the Museum*, Rexy the T-Rex skeleton looks fierce but is really quite cute and chases bones like a puppy.

▶ In *T-Rex: Back to the Cretaceous* (1998), Ally finds a mysterious egglike rock—which transports her back to the end of the Dinosaur Age.

268 In movies, *Tyrannosaurus rex* is perhaps most famous from the *Jurassic Park* series. These began with *Jurassic Park* itself in 1993, then *The Lost World: Jurassic Park* in 1997, *Jurassic Park 3* in 2001, and *Jurassic World* in 2015. *Tyrannosaurus rex* is shown breaking out of its fenced enclosure, attacking people, and generally causing havoc—but also looking after and protecting its baby with great care.

269 *Toy Story* movies, games, and other products feature an unusual *Tyrannosaurus rex* toy called "Rex" who is nervous, weedy, and worried. This is very unlike the usual fearsome character given to T-Rex.

▶ The *T-Rex* of *Jurassic Park* tries to sniff out human prey, but in the end it saves them from being attacked by marauding raptor dinosaurs.

What next for *T-Rex*?

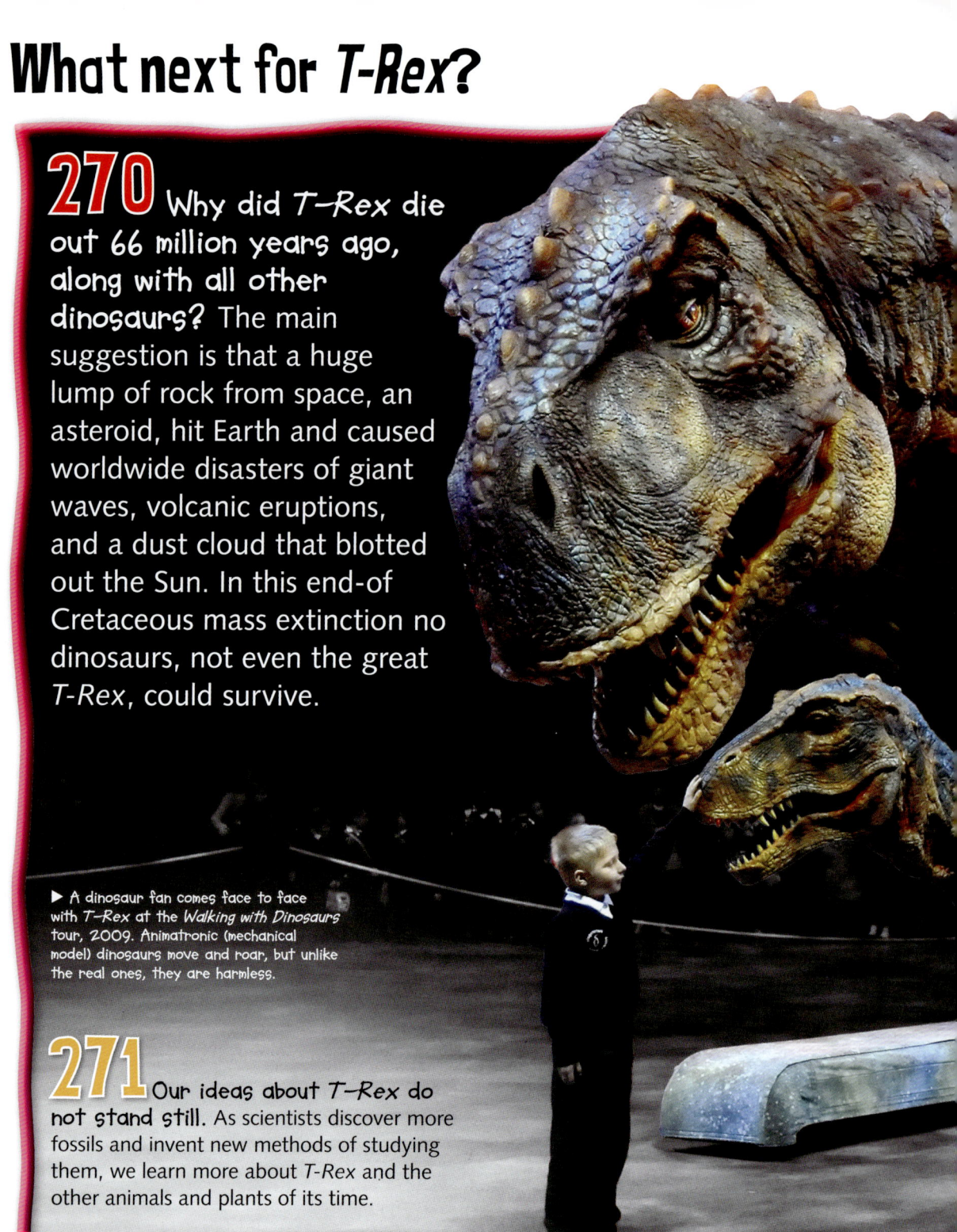

270 **Why did *T-Rex* die out 66 million years ago, along with all other dinosaurs?** The main suggestion is that a huge lump of rock from space, an asteroid, hit Earth and caused worldwide disasters of giant waves, volcanic eruptions, and a dust cloud that blotted out the Sun. In this end-of Cretaceous mass extinction no dinosaurs, not even the great *T-Rex*, could survive.

▶ A dinosaur fan comes face to face with *T-Rex* at the *Walking with Dinosaurs* tour, 2009. Animatronic (mechanical model) dinosaurs move and roar, but unlike the real ones, they are harmless.

271 **Our ideas about *T-Rex* do not stand still.** As scientists discover more fossils and invent new methods of studying them, we learn more about *T-Rex* and the other animals and plants of its time.

T-REX

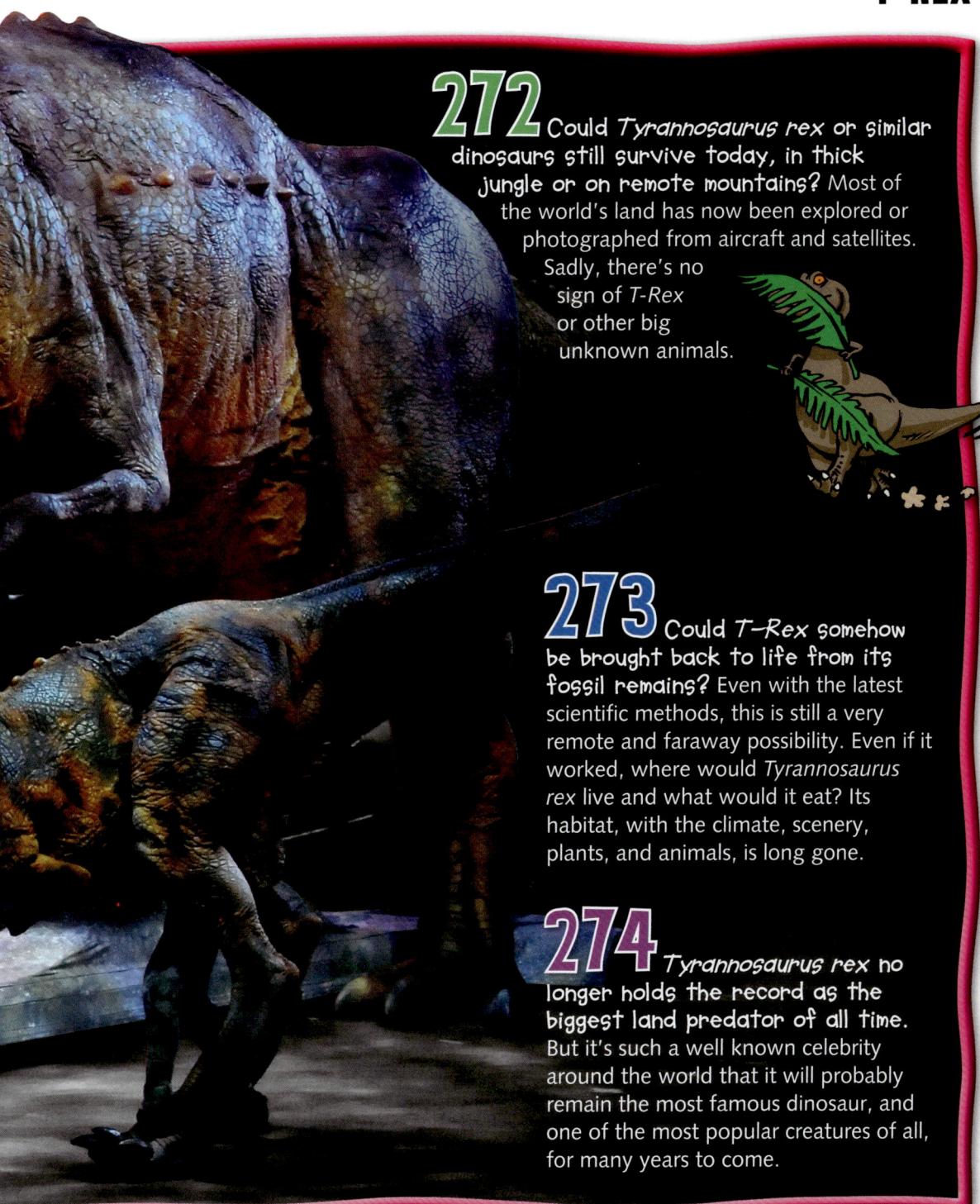

272 Could *Tyrannosaurus rex* or similar dinosaurs still survive today, in thick jungle or on remote mountains? Most of the world's land has now been explored or photographed from aircraft and satellites. Sadly, there's no sign of *T-Rex* or other big unknown animals.

273 Could *T-Rex* somehow be brought back to life from its fossil remains? Even with the latest scientific methods, this is still a very remote and faraway possibility. Even if it worked, where would *Tyrannosaurus rex* live and what would it eat? Its habitat, with the climate, scenery, plants, and animals, is long gone.

274 *Tyrannosaurus rex* no longer holds the record as the biggest land predator of all time. But it's such a well known celebrity around the world that it will probably remain the most famous dinosaur, and one of the most popular creatures of all, for many years to come.

FOSSILS

275 **Without fossils, we would know nothing about prehistoric life.** Fossils are the remains of animals and plants that died a very long time ago and became preserved in rocks. These remains are our "window on the past." They show us the amazing variety of life that thrived and then disappeared over millions of years of Earth's history.

◄ This preserved rhinoceros skeleton was found at the Ashfall Fossil Beds in Nebraska. Ash from an erupting volcano covered the area nearly 12 million years ago, burying many animals on this site.

What are fossils?

276 Fossils are the preserved remains of once living things, such as bones, teeth, and claws. Usually the remains were buried in sediments—layers of tiny particles such as sand or mud. Very slowly, the layers and the remains inside them turned into solid rock.

277 In general it takes at least 10,000 years, but usually millions, for fossils to form. So the remains of living things that are a few hundred or thousand years old, such as the bandage-wrapped mummies of pharaohs in ancient Egypt, are not true fossils.

▲ A seed cone fossil of the extinct plant *Williamsonia*.

278 Many kinds of once-living things have formed fossils. They include all kinds of animals from enormous whales and dinosaurs to tiny flies and beetles. There are fossils of plants too, from small mosses and flowers to immense trees. Even microscopic bacteria have been preserved.

◄ Teeth are very hard and so make excellent fossils—especially those from *Tyrannosaurus rex*!

FOSSILS

▶ It is unusual for thin, delicate bones, such as those of the bat *Icaronycteris*, to fossilize.

279 In most cases, fossils formed from the hard parts of living things that did not rot away soon after death. As well as bones, teeth, and claws these include shells, scales, and the bark, roots, cones, and seeds of plants.

280 Much more rarely, soft parts have been preserved as fossils, such as flower petals and worm bodies. Where this has happened, it gives a fascinating glimpse into how these ancient life-forms looked and lived.

▼ The tube worms' soft bodies soon decayed but their hard, coiled tubes were preserved in the seabed mud.

QUIZ

Which of these are true fossils?

A. A bird called the dodo, which died out over 300 years ago

B. Two-thousand-year-old pots and vases from ancient Rome

C. The first shellfish that appeared in the sea over 500 million years ago

Answer:
C is a true fossil. The others are much too recent.

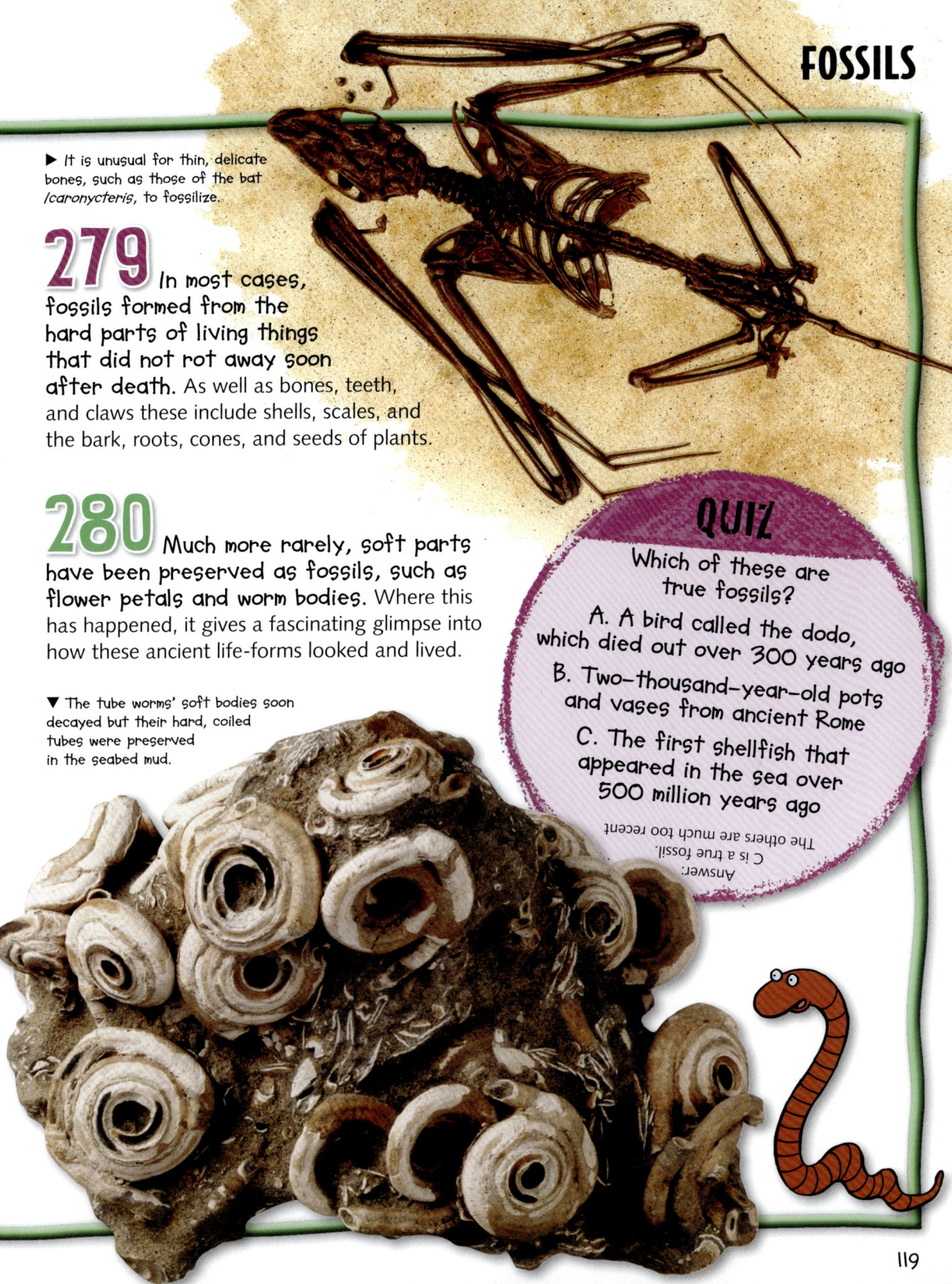

Fossils get scientific

281 **People turned to science to explain fossils.** Danish geologist (rock expert) Nicolas Steno (1638–1686) noticed that objects called "tongue stones" looked similar to the teeth of living sharks. He wondered if the teeth of ancient sharks had turned to stone.

I DON'T BELIEVE IT!
Before scientists could explain how fossils formed, bones of huge animals such as dinosaurs were thought to be from human giants—some more than 16 feet tall!

282 **French scientist Georges Cuvier (1769–1832) showed that fossils of elephants were similar to those living today.** He suggested they had become extinct—died out forever. This caused a great stir. Most people at that time believed God created animals and plants and would never let any of them die out.

▲ Nicolas Steno made sketches of the strange, pointed "rocks" he found, and saw that they were similar in shape to the teeth of living sharks.

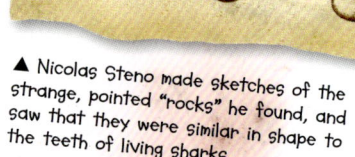

◀ Cuvier studied and named the fossil skull of the huge prehistoric sea lizard *Mosasaurus*.

283 In the 1820s, English doctor Gideon Mantell (1790–1852) found some huge fossil teeth similar to those of the iguana lizard, but bigger. He called the beast they came from *Iguanodon*. This was the first dinosaur to be named. Soon the search was on for fossils of more dinosaurs and other extinct animals.

284 In 1859, English naturalist Charles Darwin (1809–1882) published his book *On The Origin of Species*. In it, Darwin suggested that species (kinds) of living things that could not succeed in the struggle for survival died out or changed into new kinds, leaving fossils on the way.

285 During the 1800s, a new and important branch of science called paleontology began. This is the study of prehistoric life and it relies greatly on fossils of all kinds.

◀ Darwin examined fossils of the giant sloth *Megatherium* and wrote: "Existing animals have a close relation in form to extinct species."

How fossils form

▼ All living things die. Those living in water, such as this ichthyosaur, are more likely to leave fossils than those on land.

286 When a living thing dies, its flesh and other soft parts start to rot. Sometimes they are eaten by scavenging creatures such as worms and insects. The harder parts, such as teeth and bones, rot more slowly and last longer.

287 Fossil formation usually begins like this, and very often in water. Sediments tend to settle on dead animals and plants in ponds, lakes, rivers, and seas. This is the main reason why most fossils are of plants and animals that lived in water or somehow got washed into water.

1. After death, the ichthyosaur sinks to the seabed. Worms, crabs, and other scavengers eat its soft body parts.

FOSSILS

START SOME FOSSILS

You will need:
small stones   glass pitcher
sand   water

Imagine the stones are "bones" of an ancient creature. They get washed into a river—put them in the pitcher and half-fill with water. Then the "bones" are covered by sediment—sprinkle in the sand.

288 Over time, more sediment layers settle on top of the remains. As they are covered deeper, further rotting or scavenging is less likely.

289 Water trickles into the sediments and once–living remains. The water contains dissolved substances such as minerals and salts. Gradually, these replace the once-living parts and turn them and the sediments into solid rock. This is called permineralization.

290 Most living things rot away soon after death, so the chances of anything becoming a fossil are slim. Also, sedimentary rock layers change over time, becoming heated and bent, which can destroy fossils in them. The chances of anyone finding a fossil are even tinier. This is why the record of fossils in rocks represents only a tiny proportion of prehistoric life.

2. Sediments cover the hard body parts, such as bones and teeth, which gradually turn into solid rock.

3. Millions of years later the upper rock layers wear away and the fossil remains are exposed.

123

Mold and cast fossils

291 Because of the way fossils form, they are almost always found in sedimentary rocks such as sandstone, limestone, chalk, shale, and slate. Other kinds of rocks, such as igneous rocks that cool from red-hot, runny lava erupted from volcanoes, do not contain fossils.

▼ Ammonites were fierce hunting animals related to squid. They died out with the dinosaurs 65 million years ago.

Cast fossil

Mold fossil

▲ This ammonite fossil has split into part and counterpart, with a mold and cast fossil inside.

292 As the bits and pieces of sediments become solid rock, the once-living remains within them may not. They are dissolved by water and gradually washed away. The result is a hole in the rock the same shape as the remains, called a mold fossil.

293 After more time, the hole or mold in the rock may fill with minerals deposited by water. This produces a lump of stone that is different in makeup from the surrounding rocks, but is the same shape as the original remains. This is known as a cast fossil.

FOSSILS

▲ Sometimes many animals are fossilized together. Perhaps these fish were trapped when the water they were in dried up. Their remains show amazing detail.

294 Molds and casts form with a whole fossil, and also with holes and spaces within a fossil. For example, the fossil skull of an animal may have a space inside where the brain once was. If this fills with minerals it can form a lump of rock that is the same size and shape as the original brain. These types of cast fossils are known as endocasts.

295 Usually, the slower fossilization happens, the more details it preserves of the original living parts. Incredible tiny features are shown even under the microscope.

I DON'T BELIEVE IT!
Fossil skulls of the ancient humans called Neanderthals show that many of them had bigger brains than people of today!

125

Special preservation

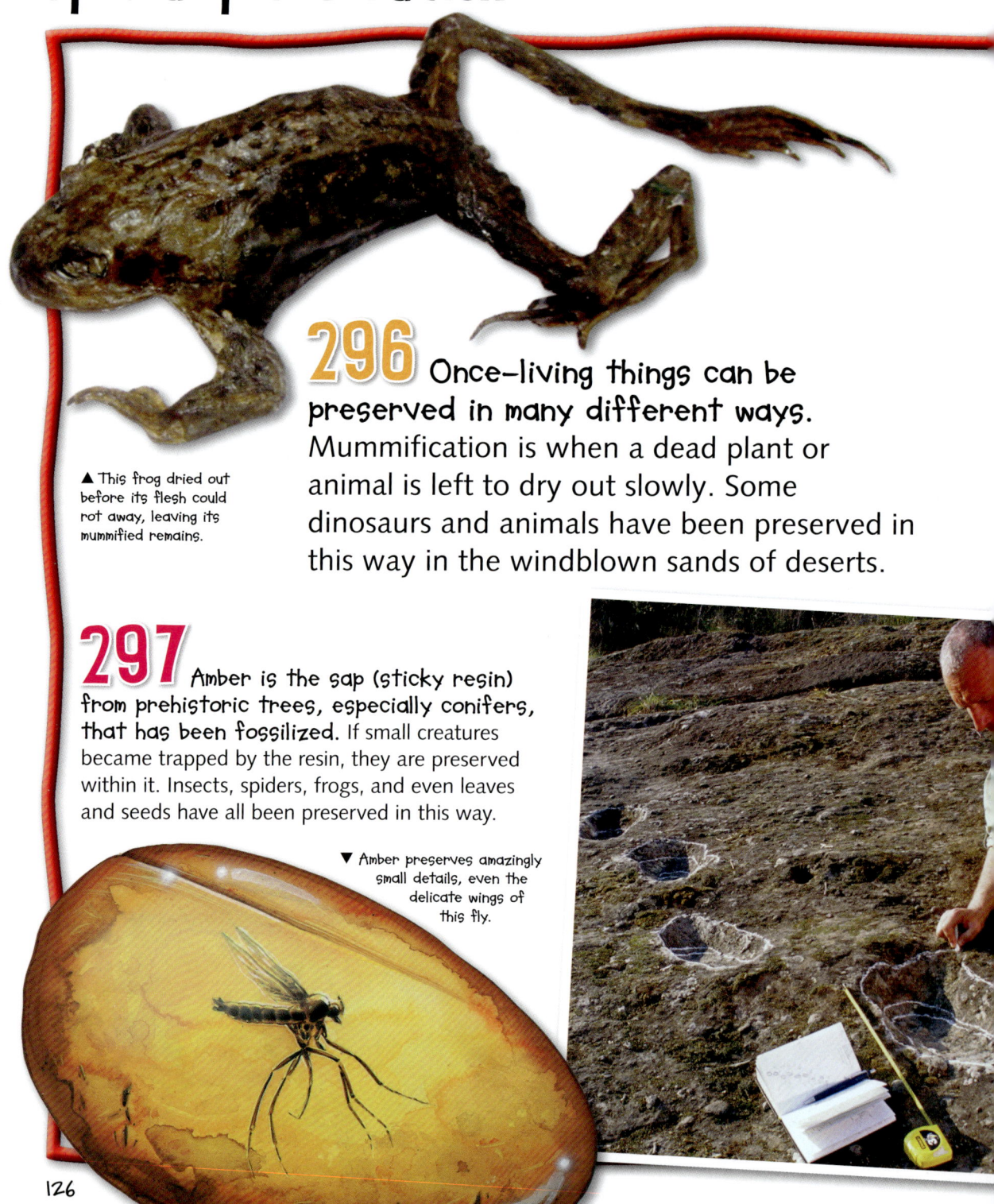

▲ This frog dried out before its flesh could rot away, leaving its mummified remains.

296 Once-living things can be preserved in many different ways. Mummification is when a dead plant or animal is left to dry out slowly. Some dinosaurs and animals have been preserved in this way in the windblown sands of deserts.

297 Amber is the sap (sticky resin) from prehistoric trees, especially conifers, that has been fossilized. If small creatures became trapped by the resin, they are preserved within it. Insects, spiders, frogs, and even leaves and seeds have all been preserved in this way.

▼ Amber preserves amazingly small details, even the delicate wings of this fly.

FOSSILS

298 Natural pools of thick, sticky tar ooze up from the ground in some places such as forests and scrubland. Animals that become trapped sink into the tar pit and may be preserved— even huge creatures such as wolves, deer, bears, sabertooth cats, and mammoths.

▶ In 1977, the perfectly preserved body of this baby mammoth was found thawing out in Siberia. The mammoth had been trapped in ice for thousands of years.

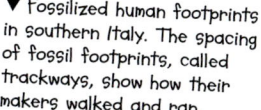

▼ Fossilized human footprints in southern Italy. The spacing of fossil footprints, called trackways, show how their makers walked and ran.

299 Being naturally frozen into the ice of the far north or south is a type of preservation. It's not true fossilization, but as the ice melts it reveals deep-frozen flowers, trees, mammoths, and deer.

MATCH-UP!

Match the following with how they were preserved.

A. Desert-living dinosaur
B. Wolf in woodland
C. Tree-dwelling insect

1. Natural tar pit
2. Trapped in amber
3. Mummification

Answers:
A3 B1 C2

300 Trace fossils are not actual body parts of once-living things. They are signs or "traces" made by them, which then became fossilized. Examples include the footprints of animals, their burrows, egg shells, teeth marks, and scratch marks, which can all turn to stone.

Fossils and time

301 Fossils are studied by many kinds of scientists. Paleontologists are general experts on fossils and prehistoric life. Paleozoologists specialize in prehistoric creatures, and paleobotanists in prehistoric plants. Geologists study rocks, soil, and other substances that make up the Earth. All of these sciences allow us to work out the immense prehistory of the Earth.

302 Earth's existence is divided into enormous lengths of time called eons, which are split into eras, then periods, epochs, and finally, stages. Each of these time divisions is marked by changes in the rocks formed at the time—and if the rocks are sedimentary, by the fossils they contain. The whole time span, from the formation of the Earth 4,600 million years ago to today, is known as the geological time scale.

▼ Starting with the Cambrian Period (far right), this timeline shows 11 major time periods in Earth's history. It gives examples of some of the fossil animals and plants that have been found for each period. "MYA" stands for "millions of years ago."

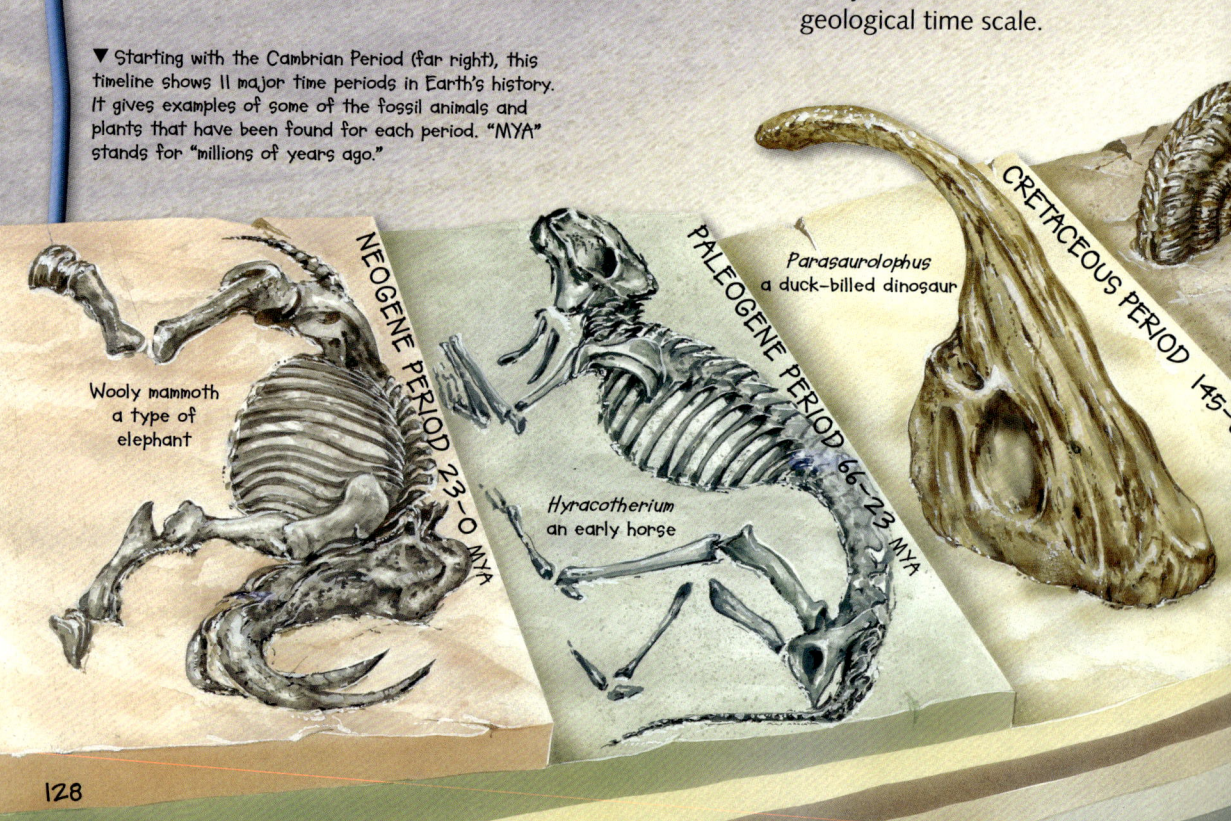

Wooly mammoth a type of elephant

NEOGENE PERIOD 23–0 MYA

Hyracotherium an early horse

PALEOGENE PERIOD 66–23 MYA

Parasaurolophus a duck-billed dinosaur

CRETACEOUS PERIOD 145–

FOSSILS

303 An example of a geological time division is the Cretaceous Period, from 145 to 66 million years ago. It is named after creta or *kreta*, a Latin word for chalk. Due to temperature, rainfall, and other climate conditions, layers of chalk rocks formed. They contained fossils such as certain kinds of shellfish, the winged reptiles known as pterosaurs, and many kinds of dinosaurs.

Trilobite — a shelled marine creature
CAMBRIAN PERIOD 542–488 MYA
ORDOVICIAN PERIOD 488–443 MYA
Graptolite — a simple marine animal
SILURIAN PERIOD 443–416 MYA
Birkenia — a type of fish
DEVONIAN PERIOD 416–359 MYA
Crinoid — a simple marine animal
CARBONIFEROUS PERIOD 359–299 MYA
Lepidodendron — a primitive tree
PERMIAN PERIOD 299–251 MYA
Diplocaulus — an early amphibian
TRIASSIC PERIOD 251–200 MYA
Rhamphorhynchus — a winged reptile
JURASSIC PERIOD 200–145.5 MYA
Stephanoceras — a type of ammonite

MAKE CHALK FOSSILS

You will need:
chalk sticks   metal teaspoon

Chalk often contains fossil shellfish. Find pictures of long, thin examples, such as razor shells, mussels, and belemnites. Use the spoon to scrape and carve the chalk sticks into shapes to make your own "fossil" museum.

Working out dates

304 **"Dating" a fossil means finding out how old it is.** Usually, rocks found deeper in the ground are older than the rock layers above them, so any fossils they contain are also older. Sedimentary rock layers and their fossils have been compared to build up a picture of which fossilized plants and animals lived when.

I DON'T BELIEVE IT!
Thousands of kinds of ammonites lived from 400–65 million years ago, and some were more than 10 feet across!

▼ Different rock layers can be clearly seen in the Grand Canyon. The layers have been revealed by the Colorado River as it winds its way through the canyon.

305 **If a new fossil is found, it can be compared with this overall pattern to get an idea of its age.** This is known as relative dating—finding the date of a fossil relative to other fossils of known ages.

FOSSILS

▲ Some types of chalk rocks are almost entirely made of the fossils of small sea creatures.

306 Certain types of plants and animals were very common, survived for millions of years, and left plenty of fossil remains. This makes them extremely useful for relative dating. They are known as marker, index, indicator, guide, or zone fossils.

307 Most index fossils come from the sea, where preservation is more likely than on land. They include multi-legged trilobites, curly-shelled ammonites, ball-shaped echinoids (sea urchins), and netlike graptolites. On land, tough pollen grains and spores from plants are useful index fossils.

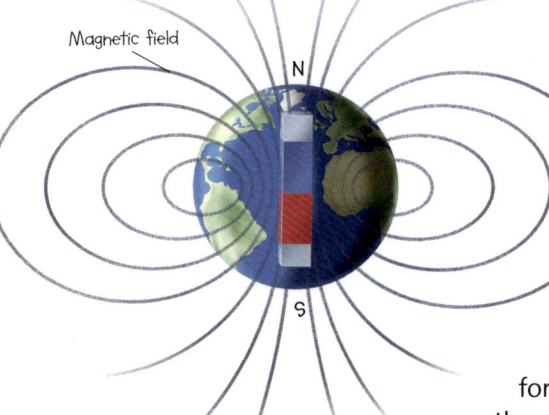
▲ Earth's magnetism has changed and even reversed over millions of years, helping to date fossils.

▶ Trilobites make good index fossils. Different kinds appeared and then died out between 530 million and about 250 million years ago.

308 Earth's natural magnetic field changed many times through prehistory. When some kinds of igneous rocks formed by cooling, the magnetism was "frozen" into them, known as paleomagnetism. It can be dated by comparison with the whole pattern of magnetic changes through Earth's history.

How many years ago?

309 Relative dating, by comparing fossils with each other, shows if one fossil is older or younger than another. But how do we know the actual age of fossils in millions of years, known as absolute dating?

I DON'T BELIEVE IT!
The oldest fossils are believed to be tiny bloblike microbes similar to today's bacteria and blue-green algae (cyanobacteria). They are more than 3,400 million years old.

310 The main kind of absolute dating is based on naturally occurring substances. These give off tiny amounts of rays and particles, known as radioactivity. As they give off these weak forms of energy, the substances—known as radioisotopes—change or "decay" slightly. The amounts of different radioisotopes in a fossil can be measured to show how long ago it formed. This is known as radiometric dating.

311 Several kinds of substances are used for radiometric dating. Each decays at a set rate, some slower than others. Very slow ones are useful for the oldest fossils, and the fastest ones for young fossils.

◀ The rocks of the Canadian Shield, a huge area of land in eastern and central Canada, have been dated to more than 2,500 million years ago.

FOSSILS

312 Radiocarbon dating is based on the change or decay of one form of carbon known as C14. It happens relatively fast and is useful for a time span up to 60,000 years ago. This helps with dating young fossils and with items such as deep-frozen mammoths.

313 In potassium–argon dating, the element potassium changes into argon very slowly, over billions of years. It's useful for rock layers formed just above or below fossils from billions of years ago to about 100,000 years ago. Rubidium-strontium and uranium-lead dating can reveal the age of even older rocks, almost back to when Earth began.

▼ Geologists measure tiny amounts of radioactivity in rocks and fossils using equipment such as Geiger counters.

▼ Radiocarbon dating.

1. Woolly mammoth eats plants containing C14

2. Mammoth dies, no more C14 is taken in

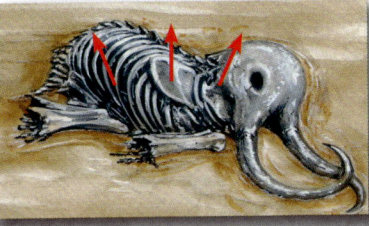
3. Half of C14 decays every 5,730 years

133

Fossil-hunting takes off

314 From the early 19th century, fossil-hunting became more popular. Towns and cities as well as rich individuals began to establish museums and collections of the "wonders of nature" with displays of stuffed animals, pinned insects, pressed flowers, and lots of fossils.

FOSSIL MATCH

Match the scientific names of these fossils with the places they were found.

A. Argentinosaurus (dinosaur)
B. Toxorhynchites mexicanus (mosquito in amber)
C. Proconsul africanus (ape-monkey)

1. Mexico, Central America
2. Argentina, South America
3. Africa

Answers:
A2 B1 C3

315 **People began to earn a living by finding and selling fossils.** One of the first was Mary Anning (1799–1847) of Lyme Regis, southern England. For many years she collected fossils from the seashore, where waves and storms regularly cracked open boulders and cliffs to reveal new finds. Mary discovered fossil fish, ichthyosaurs, plesiosaurs, pterosaurs, and many other animals.

▶ As in Mary Anning's time, fossils still appear from the rocks at Lyme Regis.

FOSSILS

316 In 1881, the British Museum opened its display of natural history collections in London, UK, showing fossils and similar wonders from around the world. Other great cities had similar museums and sent fossil-hunters to remote places for the most spectacular finds.

▲ By the 1860s many museums had fossils on display, such as this "sea serpent" or mosasaur.

▼ Cope and Marsh found and described about 130 new kinds of dinosaurs.

Othniel Charles Marsh

Edward Drinker Cope

317 Between the 1870s and 1890s, two of the leading fossil-hunters were Americans Othniel Charles Marsh and Edward Drinker Cope. Their teams tried to outdo each other to discover the most and best fossil dinosaurs, as well as other animals and plants too.

▲ The first fossil stegosaur skulls were found in the 1870s.

▶ The dinosaur *Stegosaurus* was named by Marsh in 1877.

318 From the early 1900s fossil-hunting spread to Africa and then in the 1920s to Mongolia and China. From the 1970s there were finds in South America and Australia. Today, fossil-hunters go all over the world in search of new discoveries.

Dinosaurs today

319 The name "dinosaur" was invented in 1842 by English scientist Richard Owen. He realized that the fossils of some prehistoric creatures were reptiles, but different from any known reptile group. So he made a new group, Dinosauria. Its first three members were *Iguanodon*, *Megalosaurus*, and *Hylaeosaurus*, all from fossils found in England.

▲ Fossil *Sinosauropteryx* has long legs and feet, lower left. Its tail arches up and forward to its skull, upper right.

321 In 1996 fossils of the dinosaur *Sinosauropteryx* showed it had feathers. This slim, fast meat-eater, only 3 feet long, lived 123 million years ago in China. Its feathers were thin and threadlike, not designed for flying.

▲ The dinosaur *Caudipteryx* from China had tiny arms and fanned-out tail feathers.

320 From the 1850s there was a rush to find hundreds of new dinosaurs in North America. In the 1920s exciting discoveries were made in Central Asia. Today, dinosaur remains are being found all over the world, even in frozen Antarctica. Some of the most amazing fossils in recent years come from Argentina and China.

▶ *Microraptor* was one of the smallest raptors ("thief" dinosaurs), just 32 inch long.

FOSSILS

▲ *Yutyrannus* was one of the biggest feathered dinosaurs, and weighed almost 2 tons. Its fossils are 120 million years old and come from northeast China.

▼ Macaws and other birds are flying dinosaurs of today.

322 Following *Sinosauropteryx*, many more feathered dinosaurs have been found. These include turkey-sized *Caudipteryx*, tiny *Microraptor*, 6.5 feet *Dilong*, and the huge meat-eater *Yutyrannus*, at over 30 feet in length. But none of these creatures had bodies or feathers designed for flight. However *Archaeopteryx*, which lived 150 million years ago, was a small meat-eater with wide feathers just right for flight.

323 Most experts now believe that birds evolved from small meat-eating dinosaurs. The modern scientific view is that birds are part of the dinosaur group. This means not all dinosaurs went extinct 65 million years ago. Some are alive today. They hop, flap, and sing in our gardens, parks, woods, and other habitats—they are birds.

▶ An early cousin of *Tyrannosaurus*, *Dilong* was also much smaller, about 6.5 feet from nose to tail.

324 The dinosaur with shortest name was also one of the smallest. *Mei* (meaning "sound asleep") was 24 inches long and probably covered in feathers.

▶ Fossils have been found of *Mei* sleeping in a birdlike pose. Indeed, it may be a link between dinosaurs and birds.

137

Famous hot spots

325 Some places around the world have become famous for their fossils. These places are often in the news because of dinosaur remains. However dinosaur finds are only some of the thousands of fossils being unearthed and studied.

▼ This map shows some of the most famous fossil sites around the world.

326 The Midwest "Badlands" of North America has many famous fossil sites. At Dinosaur National Monument, on the border between Colorado and Utah, the rocks date to almost 150 million years ago. Apart from dinosaur remains they also yield fossils of crocodiles, turtles, frogs, shellfish, and plants.

USA
Dinosaur National Monument

◄ Dinosaur fossils at Dinosaur National Monument. This park opened in 1915 and receives over 350,000 visitors each year.

BRAZIL
Santana Formation

327 In northeast Brazil in South America there are limestone rocks about 110–90 million years old known as the Santana Formation. Detailed fossils include pterosaurs, reptiles, frogs, insects, and plants. Some fossil fish were preserved with the remains of their last meals inside their bodies.

◄ This 100-million-year-old dragonfly is one of thousands from Brazil's Santana Formation rocks.

FOSSILS

328 Some of the best European fossils come from limestone quarries around Solnhofen, southern Germany. There are dinosaurs, pterosaurs, the earliest known bird *Archaeopteryx*, fish, insects, and softbodied jellyfish.

▲ One of the smallest dinosaurs, *Compsognathus* has been preserved in amazing detail at Solnhofen, Germany.

329 Lightning Ridge is in northwest New South Wales, Australia. As well as beautiful black opal gemstones there are fossils 110 million years old of long-gone mammals, dinosaurs, pterosaurs, crocodiles, turtles, sharks, crayfish, snails, shellfish, and pine cones.

330 Fayoum, south of Cairo in Egypt, is one of Africa's best fossil sites. There are remains 40–25 million years old of prehistoric mammals such as hippos, rhinos, elephants, rats, bats, monkeys, and even whales.

▲ Fossils of more than 400 whales such as *Basilosaurus* are known from Egypt's Fayoum area.

▲ Fossils of the giant wombat *Diprotodon* have been found in Australia.

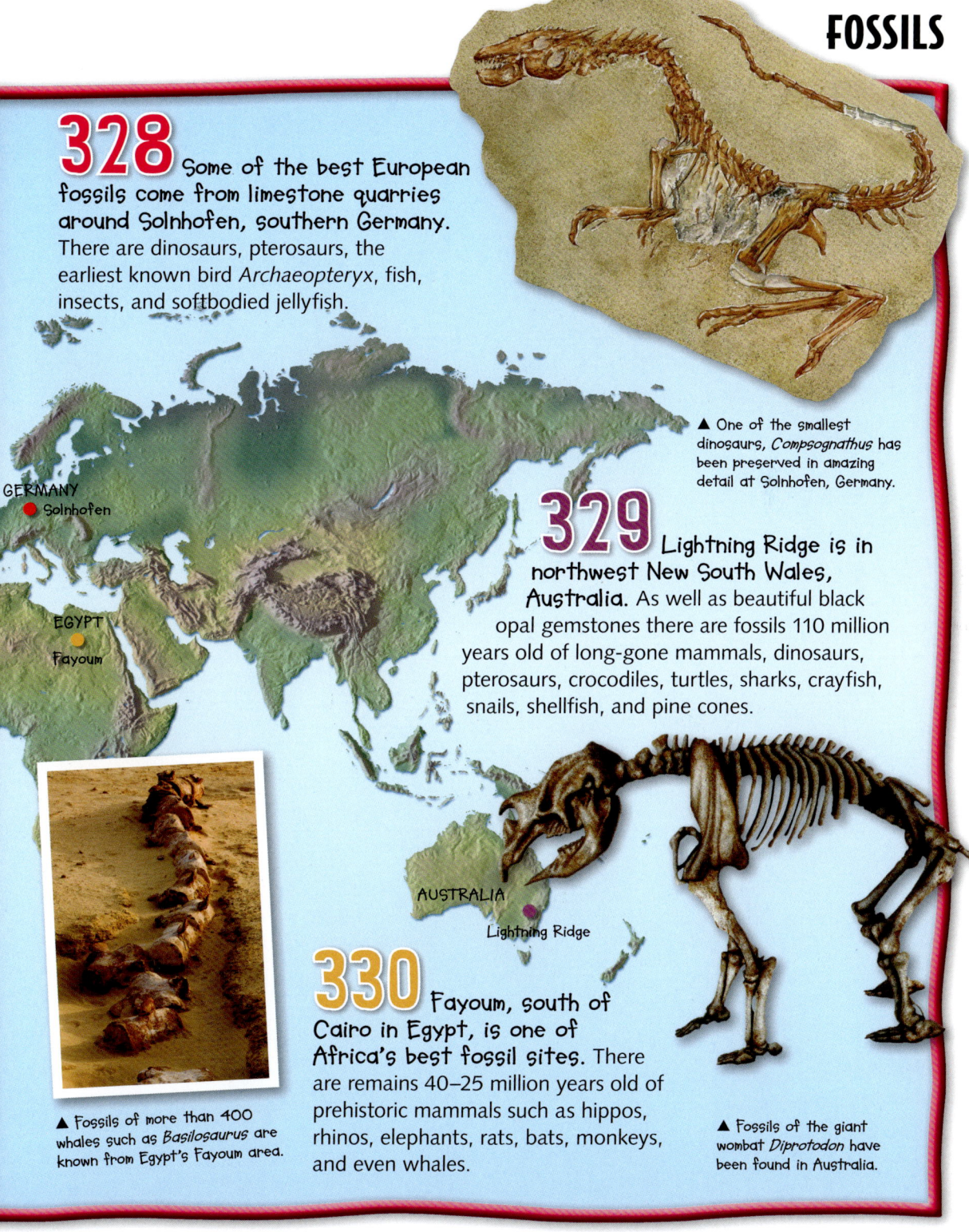

Looking for fossils

331 **Where do we find fossils?** Fossil-hunters use many kinds of aids and clues to find the best sites. Geological maps show which kinds of rocks are found at or just under the surface. To contain fossils, these rocks need to be sedimentary, such as limestone.

PLAN A FOSSIL DIG
You will need:
pencil and notebook
pictures of fossil dig sites

You're in charge of a fossil-finding trip to a remote desert. Make a list of the equipment and supplies you think you'll need. Look through the pages of this book for clues. Once you have a list, draw a plan of your dig and decide who to take with you.

332 **Fossil-hunters are careful to get permission to search a site.** The landowner, land manager, and local authorities must all agree on the search methods and the ownership of any finds. This avoids problems such as trespassing, criminal damage, and "fossil-rustling" (stealing).

▶ Paleontologists sift through rocks and common fossils for signs of important specimens at Bromacker Quarry, Germany.

▶ Year after year sun, wind, rain, and ice wear away rocks and reveal fossils at Dinosaur Provincial Park, Alberta, Canada.

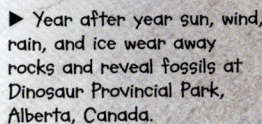 **Good places to look for fossils are where rocks are regularly broken apart and worn away by waves, wind, sun, ice, and other weather.** This is the process of erosion. It happens at cliffs, seashores, river banks, and valleys, canyons, and caves. It also happens where people dig quarries, mines, road and railway cuttings, and building foundations.

334 **Satellite images, aerial photographs, survey trips by plane, or even just walking around show the nature of the ground.** Bare rocky areas are best, rather than areas covered with soil, plants, and trees.

▶ This satellite photo of East Africa's Olduvai Gorge shows one of the world's best areas for prehistoric human fossils.

335 **Fossil-hunters also follow a code of guidelines.** These show how to cause the least damage when digging, how to stay safe, and how to restore the site afterward. They need to be aware that laws and regulations about fossil-hunting vary from state to state too, and also depend on whether the dig is on federal land or not.

141

At the dig

336 Some people look for fossils in their spare time and if they find one it's a bonus. At an important site, scientists such as paleontologists organize an excavation or "dig" that can last for many months.

I DON'T BELIEVE IT!
A fossil leg bone from a huge dinosaur, being solid rock, can weigh more than one ton!

337 The dig area is divided into squares called a grid, usually by string or strips of wood. This is used to record the positions of the finds. As the excavation continues, the workers make notes, take photographs, draw sketches, and use many other recording methods.

▼ Paleontologists dig up fossil mammoth remains in California. The valuable specimens are wrapped in layers of sacking and plaster before being moved.

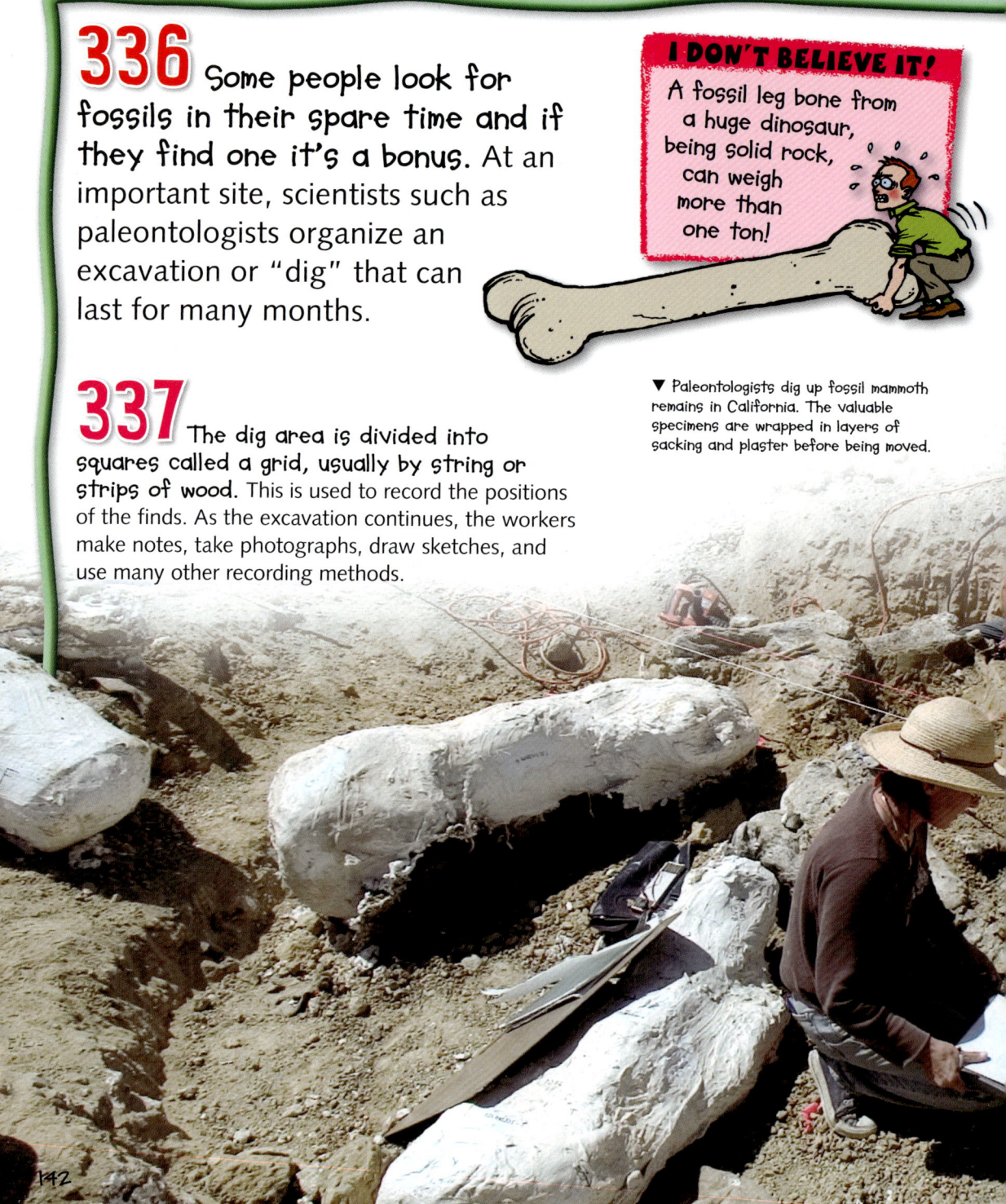

338 At first there may be lots of loose rocks, boulders, or soil to remove, called overburden. Big, powerful tools might be used such as mechanical diggers, road drills (jackhammers), or even dynamite!

▲ It can take weeks to clean a large fossil such as this elephant skull and tusk.

339 As fossils are exposed, experts decide whether they are worth digging out. Gradually the excavation methods become more careful, using hammers, chisels, small picks, and brushes to avoid damaging the find. It can be a lengthy, difficult task. The dig site might be a baking desert, tropical swamp, or freezing mountainside.

340 Small bits of loose rock might be sieved to find tiny fossils. Soft, fragile fossils can be covered with material such as plaster or fiberglass, which hardens into a protective jacket. This allows the fossil to be lifted out.

Cleaning up fossils

341 When fossils reach the workroom, which might be in a museum or university, experts decide which ones to prepare. This means cleaning away unwanted bits of rock and stone around the fossil (the matrix) without damaging the fossil itself.

WHAT ORDER?

List these tools and equipment in the order you would use them to find, dig up, and clean a rare fossil.

A. Wooden toothpick
B. Hammer and chisel
C. Stick of dynamite
D. Soft-bristled paintbrush
E. Dentist's drill

Answer:
C B E A D

342 Many kinds of tools and equipment are needed to clean or expose a fossil. They range from small hammers, chisels, and drills, to engraving tools, pins and picks, sanders, files, and different brushes. The preparator (person working on the fossil) stops regularly to examine the specimen and decide which part to clean next.

▶ Museum preparators work carefully to remove unwanted bits of rock and leave only the fossil.

FOSSILS

343 Microscopes are often used to show tiny details of a fossil during preparation. Usually this is a stereoscopic microscope with two eyepieces, like binoculars, mounted on a stand with the specimen beneath.

▶ It may take a year to dissolve rock with acid and expose the fossils— these are unhatched dinosaur eggs.

▲ The enlarged view through a stereo microscope shows lots of detail, to avoid scratching or chipping the specimen.

Dinosaur embryo

344 When the fossil is one type of rock and the matrix is another, preparators may use chemicals to expose the fossil. Different acids are tested on small parts of the matrix and fossil, to see if they dissolve the former but not the latter.

345 Very few animals or plants die neatly in one piece and are preserved whole. So it's incredibly rare to find a whole fossilized plant or animal with all the parts positioned as they were in life. Most fossils are bits and pieces that are crushed and distorted. Putting them back together is very difficult!

On display

346 **In a well organized fossil collection, specimens are given catalog numbers showing where and when they were found.** They are studied, described, and identified, and logged into a computer database or card index. Then the specimen can be easily recognized.

347 **Usually only exceptional fossils are chosen to display in museums, galleries, and exhibitions.** They might be very large for their kind, preserved in great detail, be extremely rare, found by a famous fossil-hunter, or simply very beautiful.

▼ London's Natural History Museum in the UK has some of the world's best fossil displays. The *Diplodocus* skeleton cast affectionately known as "Dippy" arrived in the capital in 1905 and delighted visitors for decades.

348 **Fossil displays vary hugely.** Some are shelves or cabinets with simple labels. Others have fossils and reconstructions of the original animals or plants, set into a realistic scene. They may have special lighting, descriptions, and diagrams, and even press-button video shows.

349 Some fossils are so rare, delicate, or valuable that they are not displayed—copies are. Copies or replicas of very rare fossils might be sent to other museums so more people can study them.

▼ The Field Museum of Natural History in Chicago, Illinois, houses a collection of 30 million geological and biological specimens and cultural objects, and large dinosaur fossil casts are star attractions.

I DON'T BELIEVE IT!

In 2002, experts reexamined the fossil jaws of a tiny creature called *Rhyniognatha* found in 1919. They realized it was probably the earliest known insect, and that it was almost 400 million years old.

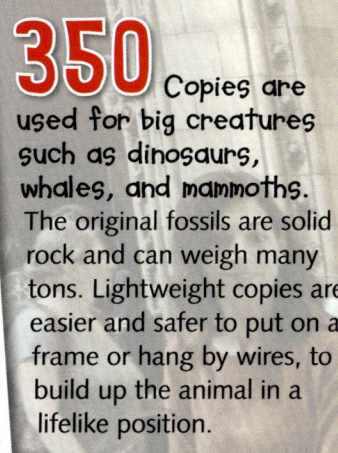

350 Copies are used for big creatures such as dinosaurs, whales, and mammoths. The original fossils are solid rock and can weigh many tons. Lightweight copies are easier and safer to put on a frame or hang by wires, to build up the animal in a lifelike position.

Fossils come alive!

351 One of the most exciting parts of fossil study is to reconstruct (rebuild) the original plant or animal. This needs a detailed knowledge of anatomy, or body structure. For example, fossils of prehistoric birds are compared to the same body parts of similar birds alive today. This is called comparative anatomy.

352 Tiny marks or "scars" on fossil bones show where the animal's muscles attached in real life. These help to reveal muscle shapes and arrangements so experts can gradually put the flesh on the (fossil) bones.

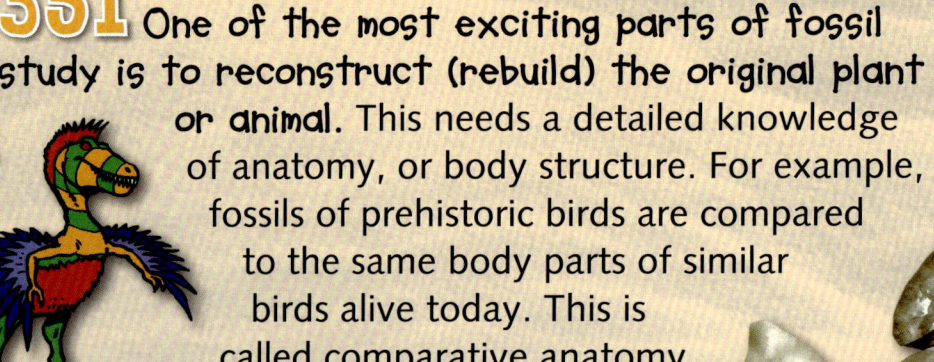

Fossil bones
Faint scars on fossil bones can help scientists work out how and where muscles were attached.

▲ This reconstruction of an ankylosaur, an armored dinosaur, is being done head first. The tail is still bare fossils of the bones.

353 We can see how a living creature walks, runs, and jumps using the joints between its bones. If fossil bones have their joints preserved, their detailed shapes and designs show the range of motion and how the animal moved.

MULTI-COLORED BIRD

You will need:
pictures of *Archaeopteryx*   color pens
tracing paper   white paper

No one knows what color the first bird *Archaeopteryx* was. Look at pictures of it in books and on websites. See how its feather colors and patterns differ. Trace an outline of *Archaeopteryx* from a book and color it to your own amazing design.

FOSSILS

Soft tissues
Flesh, guts, and muscles can be added to the skeleton as scientists compare the fossil to similar living animals.

Skin
The external covering of skin, scales, horns, and claws are added by studying fossil examples and using intelligent guess work.

354 Gradually, soft parts such as the guts of an animal or the petals of a flower, can be guessed and added to the reconstruction. Again, experts use information from fossil relatives and living cousins.

355 The outward appearance of an animal might be known from fossils such as an outer shell, scaly skin, feathers, or fur. However fossils are not original living parts—they have changed to rock. So the color of fossil skin is the color of the type of rock, not the animal. Experts guess at colors and patterns for their reconstructions.

Trading, stealing, faking

356 Fossils are big business. Thousands of people work at digs, in workrooms and in museums, exhibitions and galleries. A find such as a new dinosaur can hit the news headlines and make the discoverer famous – and rich!

357 The biggest, most complete fossil *Tyrannosaurus rex* was found in 1990 near Faith, Dakota, by Sue Hendrickson. The dinosaur was nicknamed 'Sue' and there was a long legal dispute about who owned it. Finally it was sold to the Field Museum of Chicago for more than seven million dollars!

◄ Street traders offer fossils for sale in North Africa. There is no guarantee the fossils came from the local area.

FOSSILS

I DON'T BELIEVE IT!
In 2008, a 7-metre-long fossil *Triceratops* dinosaur went on sale for £400,000 along with a fossil skull of a sabre-tooth cat for £35,000.

▶ Chinese palaeontologist Dong Zhiming with some smuggled dinosaur eggs. Every year police, customs and security staff uncover illegal collections such as this.

358 Real fossils, replicas and models are sold around the world by museums, shops, mail-order catalogues and on the Internet. Buyers range from leading museums to individuals who like the idea of a home fossil collection without the trouble of digging them up.

▼ Rare or unusual fossils, such as this ammonite shell showing detailed internal structure, can fetch huge sums of money at auction.

359 Stealing and faking fossils has been going on for centuries. In 1999 scientists announced a fossil creature called *Archaeoraptor* that seemed to be part-bird and part-dinosaur. *Archaeoraptor* showed how small meat-eating dinosaurs evolved into birds. However further study revealed that the specimen was indeed part-dinosaur and part-bird, because it was a fake with separate fossils cleverly glued together.

Famous fossils

360 Many fossils and prehistoric sites around the world are massive attractions, visited by millions of people. The Petrified Forest National Park in Arizona, USA has hundreds of huge fossilized trees and smaller specimens of animals such as dinosaurs, dating from about 225 million years ago. It receives more than half a million visitors yearly.

▲ The coelacanth is known as a 'living fossil', meaning it is very similar to its long-extinct relatives.

361 The coelacanth fish was known only from fossils and thought to have been extinct for more than 60 million years. In 1938 a living coelacanth was caught off southeast Africa and more have been discovered since. Living things that are very similar to their prehistoric relatives are known as 'living fossils'.

▶ Thousands of fossil tree trunks and branches litter the ground at Arizona's Petrified Forest National Park.

FOSSILS

362 There are only about ten fossils of *Archaeopteryx*, the first known bird. They all come from the Solnhofen area of southern Germany. They are amazingly detailed and almost priceless.

▶ Each specimen of *Archaeopteryx* is closely guarded.

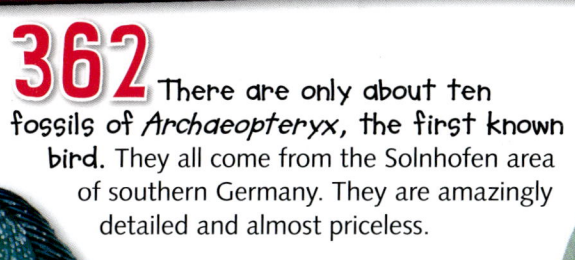

363 'Lucy' is a fossilized part-skeleton from a very early human-type creature. It was discovered in 1974 in Ethiopia, Africa and dates back about 3.2 million years. Thousands of people flock to see 'her' every year.

◀ Piltdown Man was really the skull of a human from about 500 years ago combined with the jawbone of an orang-utan.

364 Piltdown Man is perhaps the most famous fossil fake. It was found in southeast England in 1912 and thought to be an early kind of human. In 1953 it was exposed as a hoax by new scientific methods.

I DON'T BELIEVE IT!

Animal droppings can become fossils known as coprolites. Leftovers in them can show what an animal ate. Luckily they are no longer squishy and smelly, but have become solid rock.

153

Looking to the future

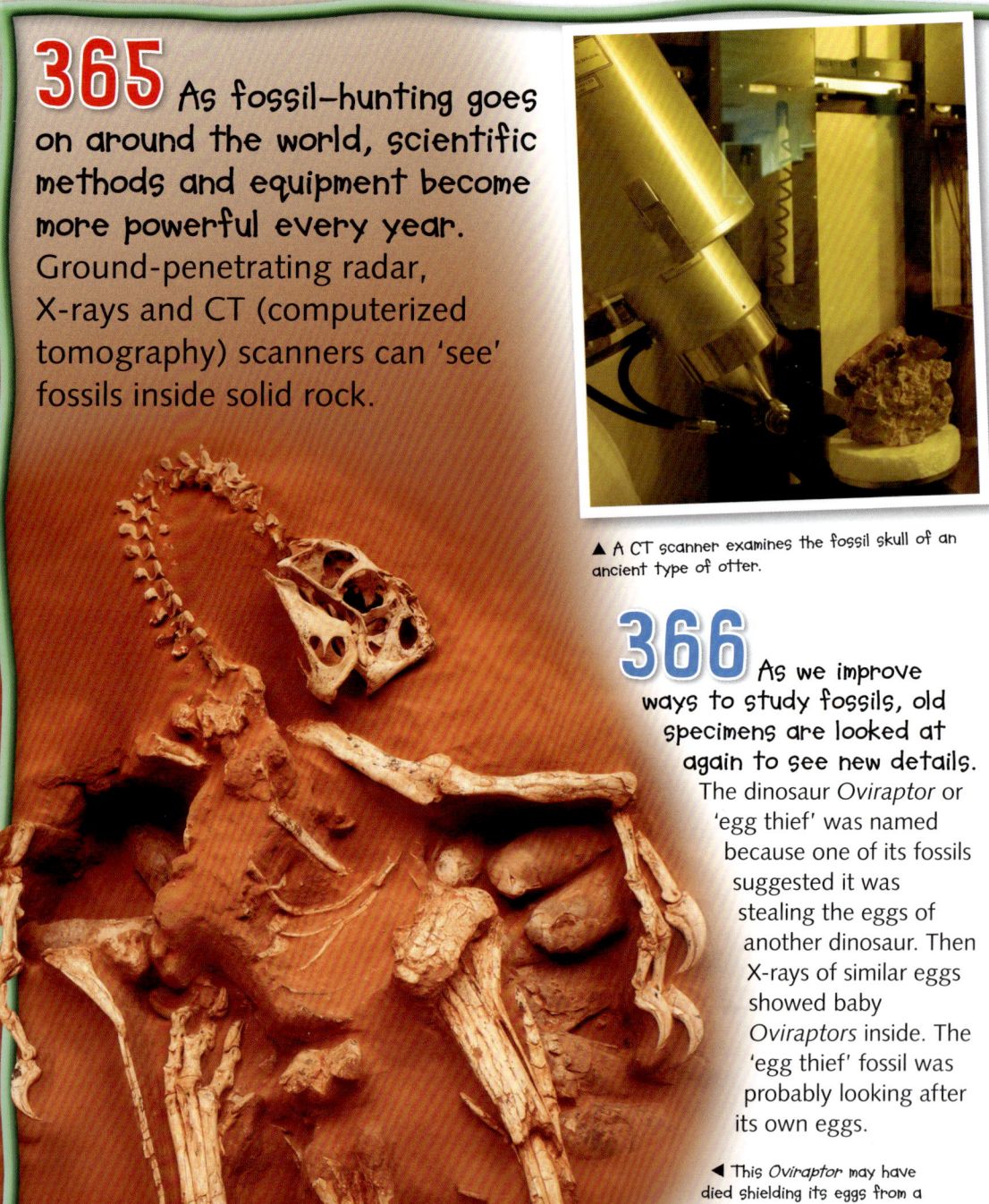

365 As fossil-hunting goes on around the world, scientific methods and equipment become more powerful every year. Ground-penetrating radar, X-rays and CT (computerized tomography) scanners can 'see' fossils inside solid rock.

▲ A CT scanner examines the fossil skull of an ancient type of otter.

366 As we improve ways to study fossils, old specimens are looked at again to see new details. The dinosaur *Oviraptor* or 'egg thief' was named because one of its fossils suggested it was stealing the eggs of another dinosaur. Then X-rays of similar eggs showed baby *Oviraptors* inside. The 'egg thief' fossil was probably looking after its own eggs.

◄ This *Oviraptor* may have died shielding its eggs from a predator, 75 million years ago.

367 **Some amazing fossils of the 1990s–2000s are from Liaoning Province in northeast China.** Dated to 130 million years ago, they show details of creatures and plants, including dinosaurs with feathers and a cat-sized mammal that preyed on baby dinosaurs.

▲ Fossils of the tiny feathered dinosaur *Microraptor* have been found in China.

368 **New fossils provide more evidence for evolution, such as how fish changed gradually into land animals.** *Panderichthys* was a fish-like creature from 380 million years ago. It had features such as finger-like bones developing in its fins.

369 **Important fossil discoveries cause news and excitement around the world.** They affect our ideas about prehistoric life, how Earth has changed through time, evolution and extinction. They can also help to fill in the details of where we came from.

NAME GAME

Match these nicknames of fossils with their scientific names.
A. 'Lucy' B. 'Stan' C. 'Jaws'
D. 'Spike'

1. *Triceratops* (dinosaur)
2. *Megalodon* (giant shark)
3. *Australopithecus afarensis* (early human)
4. *Tyrannosaurus* (dinosaur)

Answers:
A3 B4 C2 D1

▲ *Panderichthys* was about one metre long. Its fossils come from Latvia in northeastern Europe.

155

Index

Entries in **bold** refer to main subject entries. Entries in *italics* refer to illustrations

A
absolute dating 132
Acanthostega **14**, *14*
Age of Dinosaurs **44–45**
  end **72–73**
Albertosaurus 78, 99, **100**, **101**
Alectrosaurus 99, *100*
algae **8**
alligators 74
Allodesmus **37**
Allosaurus 44, **58**, *59*, 79, 99
Alxasaurus 57
amber fossils **126**, *126*
ammonites **11**, *11*, 124, 129, 130, 131, *152*
ammonoid *63*
amphibians 14, **15**, 18, **44**
Anancus **33**
anatomy 148
Andrewsarchus **29**, *29*, **81**
ankylosaurs 67, *148*
Anning, Mary **134**, *134*
Anomalocaris 8, *8*, **9**
Apatosaurus **57**, *57*
  teeth **53**, *53*
apes **40–41**
Aphaneramma **15**
Appalachiosaurus 99, *100*
Archaeopteryx **23**, *23*, 137, **153**, *153*
Archaeoraptor 151
Archelon 63
archosaurs **47**
Ardipithecus **40**, *40*
Argentavis **38**, *38*
Argentinosaurus 54, **111**
armored dinosaurs **66–67**, 91, *148*
Arsinoitherium **29**, *29*, 74
Arthropleura **14**, *14*
arthropods 10, 14
Ashfall Fossil Beds *117*
aurochs 7
Austroraptor 43
Aviatyrannis **96**, *99*
Avimimus 78

B
baby dinosaurs **69**, *69*, **70–71**, 94, *94*

backboned animals 11
bacteria fossils 8, 118, 132
"Badlands" 138
bark fossils 119
Barosaurus **44**, 54
Baryonyx **57**
  teeth **53**, *53*
Basilosaurus 139, *139*
bat fossils 139
bear fossils 127
beetle fossils 118
Beipiaosaurus 57
belemnoid *63*
birds 23, 38, **63**, 137, *137*, 139
Birkenia 129
bone fossils 119
Brachiosaurus 54, **55**, *55*, 68, **79**, 80, *111*
brain fossil 125
  Tyrannosaurus rex **85**, *85*
Branchiosaurus 18
Branisella 74
Brontotherium **28**, *28*
Brown, Barnum 102, **103**, *103*
Bunyip 39
burrow fossils 127

C
Cambrian Period *128*, *129*
camels 35
carbon 14, 133
Carboniferous Period *129*
Carcharodontosaurus **58**, *58*, 111, **111**
cast fossils **124**, *124*, 125
cats 36
Caudipteryx *136*, 137
cave bears **37**, *37*
cave lion 6
Cenozoic Era 44, 45
ceratopsian dinosaurs 67
chalk 124
Charnia **9**, *9*
Chasmatosaurus **21**, *21*
chimpanzees 41
Chriacus 74
claws,
  dinosaurs **56–57**
  fossils 119
Climatius **12**, *12*
coelacanth 152
Coelophysis **65**, *65*
Columbian mammoth **33**, *33*

comparative anatomy 104, 148
Compsognathus 99, *99*, *139*
cone fossil *118*, 119, 139
Confuciusornis **23**, *23*
conifer fossils 126
continental drift 19
Cooksonia **9**, *9*
Cope, Edward Drinker 102, *102*, 135, *135*
coprolites **91**, *91*, 153
coral 9
Coryphodon 74
Corythosaurus 78
crayfish fossils 139
creodonts 27
Cretaceous Period 45, 62, 78, 79, *128*, 129
Cretoxyrhina 63
Crinoid *129*
crocodiles 46, 47, 74
  fossils 138, 139
CT scanners 154
Cuvier, Georges 120
cyanobacteria 132
Cynognathus **21**, *21*

D
Daphoenodon 30
Darwin, Charles 121
Daspletosaurus **101**, *101*
dating fossils **130–133**
deer **35**
  fossils 127
Deinonychus 45, **56**, *56*, 79, 99
Devonian Period *129*
"digs" **140–143**
"Dippy" 146
Diictodon **17**, *17*
Dilong **98**, *98*, 99, 137, *137*
Dimetrodon **20**, *20*, **46**, *46*
Dinictis **36**
Dinohyus **30**, *30*
Dinosaur National Monument 138
Dinosaur Provincial Park, Canada *141*
Dinosauria 136
dinosaurs **42**
  early **48–49**
  end of **72–73**
  first 47, **50–51**
  growth **94–95**
Diplocaulus 44, *129*

Diplodocus 54, **55**, 71, 146
Diprotodon 139
DNA 41
dogs **36**
Dong Zhining *151*
dragonflies *138*
  fossils *138*
dromaeosaurs *99*
Dryopithecus **40**, *40*
duck-billed dinosaurs 52, *61*, 78
Dunkleosteus **13**

E
echinoids 131
Edmontonia 78
Edmontosaurus teeth **52**, *52*
egg shell fossils 127
"egg thief" 154
eggs,
  dinosaur **68–69**, 70, 94, *94*, 145, *151*
  reptiles 16
Elasmosaurus **24**, *25*, *63*
elephants **32–33**
  fossils 120, 139
endocasts 125
entelodonts **30**
Eobasileus 74
Eogyrinus **15**
Eohippus see *Hyracotherium*
eons 128
Eoraptor **48**, *48*
Eotyrannus **96**, *99*
epochs 128
eras 128
erosion 141
Erythrosuchus **46**, *46*
Euoplocephalus **67**, *67*, *78*, 91
Euparkeria **47**, *47*
Eusthenopteron **13**, *13*
evolution 6, 16, 155
  dinosaurs 49
  humans 40
extinction 16, 120
  mass **74**, 114

F
faking fossils 150–151
Fayoum, Egypt 139
feathers 136, *136*, 137, 155
  dinosaurs *43*, *56*, 98, *98*, *104*
  first birds 23

Field Museum of Natural History *147*, 150
fish,
  first **12**
  fossils 134, 138, 139, 155
  lobefin **13**
flightless birds 38
flower fossils 118
fly fossils 118, *126*
flying reptiles *63*, 74
footprint fossils 54, *54*, *55*, 89, *127*
fossil sites **138–139**, *138–139*
fossils 8, *11*, 52, **116–119**
  collecting 146–147
  dating **130–133**
  dinosaur babies **69**, *69*, 70, 71
  excavation 142–143
  footprints 54, *54*, *55*, 89, *127*
  formation **122–123**
  geological time scale **128–129**
  hunting 140–143
  preparing 144–145
  reconstructing **148–149**
  rustling 140
  sea creatures 25
  senses 60
  stomach stones 55
  Tyrannosaurus rex **102–103**, 108–109
frog fossils 126, 138
frozen preservation 127
fungi 8
fur,
  early mammals 23
  mammal-like reptiles 47
  therapsid dinosaurs 21
Futalognkosaurus 54, 55, *55*

G
Gallimimus **53**, *53*
Gastornis 74
Geiger counter *133*
genes 41
geological time scale **128–129**
Gerrothorax **14**
giant sloth *121*
giant wombat *139*
Giganotosaurus **58**, *58*, **110**
Gigantopithecus **41**, *41*
Gorgosaurus 99, **100**, *100*
gorillas 41
Grand Canyon *130*

graptolites *129*, 131
great apes 41
grid 142
growth of dinosaurs **94–95**
Guanlong **98**, *98*, 99
guide fossils 131

H
hadrosaurs 70, 78
Hemicyclapsis **12**
Hendrickson, Sue 150
herds of dinosaurs 54, **91**
Herrerasaurus **48**, *48*, 79
Hesperocyon **36**, *36*
Hesperornis *63*
hippo fossils 139
hoofed mammals 26, 34
horses **34**, 35
human evolution 40
human fossils *141*
Hylaeosaurus 136, 138
Hylonomus **17**, *17*
Hypsilophodon **56**
Hyracotherium (*Eohippus*) **34**, *34*, 74, 128

I
Icaronycteris 119, *119*
Ice Age 37
ice ages 6, 7, 32
Ichthyornis **63**, *63*
ichthyosaur **62**, 81, *122*
  fossils 134
Ichthyosaurus *63*
Ichthyostega **15**, *15*
Iguanodon **57**, 121, 136
  teeth *121*
imperial mammoth 80, *80*
index fossils **130**, *130*, 131
indicator fossils 131
insects 14
  fossils 126, 138, 139, 147

J
jawless fish **12**, *12*
jellyfish 9
  fossils 139
Jenghizkhan **97**
Jurassic Period 44, 79, *129*

K
kangaroo 38
Kronosaurus *63*, 81

L

Lagosuchus **47**
Lambeosaurus 78
Leaellynasaura 60, *60*
leaf fossils 126
Leptictidium **26**, *26*
Lessemasaurus 49, *49*
Liaoning Province, China 155
lichens **8**
life, beginning of 8–9
Lightning Ridge, Australia 139
limestone 124, 140
Liopleurodon 81
living fossils 154
lizards 74
lobefin fish **13**
"Lucy" 153
Lyme Regis, England 134, *134*
Lystrosaurus **19**, *19*, 44

M

magnetism 131
Maiasaura **70**, *70*
Mamenchisaurus 54
mammal-like reptiles **47**
mammals **26–27**, 45, 75, *75*
  evolution 21
  first 23
  fossils 139, 155
mammoth,
  Columbian **33**, *33*
  imperial 80, *80*
  wooly 7, **32**, *32*, 128, *133*
mammoth fossils 127
Mantell, Gideon 121
Mapusaurus **111**
Marasuchus **47**
marker fossil 131
Marsh, Othniel Charles 135, *135*
marsupials **37**, 38
mass extinctions **16**, 74, 114
Massospondylus 68
Mastodonsaurus **18**, *18*
meat-eating dinosaurs **58–59**, 78, 79, 82
Megacerops 45
Megaloceros 7, **35**, *36*
Megalosaurus 136
Megatherium 121
Megazostrodon **23**, *23*
Mei 137, *137*
Mesozoic Era 44–45, 78, 79
Microraptor 136, 137, *137*, 155

millipedes 14
Moeritherium **32**
monkeys 40
  fossils 139
mosasaurs **63**, 74, *135*
Mosasaurus **22**, *22*, *63*, *120*
Moschops **19**, *19*
moss fossils 118
mold fossils **124**, *124*, 125
molds 8
movies **112–113**, *112*, *113*
mummification **126**, *126*
muscle scars 148
Muttaburrasaurus **65**, *65*

N

Nanotyrannus **97**, *98*, *109*
Natural History Museum, London, UK *146*
Neanderthal people 37, 125
Neogene Period 45, *128*
Nesodon 45
nests of dinosaurs **68**, *68*, *69*, 70, *70*
Nothronychus 57

O

Olduvai Gorge, Africa *141*
On the Origin of Species 121
orangutan 41
Ordovician Period *129*
ornithischian dinosaurs 82
ornithomimosaur dinosaurs 64
Ornithomimus **64**, *64*
ornithopod dinosaurs 65
Osborn, Henry Fairfield 102, 103
ostrich-dinosaur (*Gallimimus*) **53**, *53*
otter 31
Ottoia 10
Ouranosaurus **62**, 63
overburden 143
Oviraptor **68**, *68*, 154, *154*
Owen, Richard 136

P

Pakicetus **26**, *26*
Palaeotherium **26**, *26*
Paleogene Period 45, *128*
paleomagnetism 131
paleontologists **128**, 142, *142*
paleontology 121
Paleozoic Era 44

Panderichthys 155, *155*
Paraceratherium **39**, *39*, *74*
Parasaurolophus **61**, *61*, *78*, *90*, *128*
Patriofelis **27**
people, early 37
periods 128
Permian Period 44, *129*
permineralization 123
Petrified Forest National Park 152
pharaohs 118
Pikaia 11
Piltdown Man 153
pine cones fossils 139
placoderms **12**
Placodus **22**
plants,
  first **8**
  fossils 118, 119, 131, 138
  land 8, **9**
Plateosaurus **50**, *50*, **70**
Platybelodon **32**
Plesiadapis **40**, *40*, *74*
Plesictis **31**
plesiosaurs **62**, 74
  fossils 134
pliosaurs 81
pollen grains 131
Potamotherium **31**, *31*
potassium-argon dating 133
predator dinosaurs 92, 93
Prenocephale 92
primates **40**
Procompsognathus 44
Procoptodon **38**
prosauropods 51
Protoceratops **69**, *69*
Protosuchus **20**, *20*
Psittacosaurus **71**, *71*
Pteranodon **24**, *24*, *63*
pterosaurs 24, 25, 47, **63**, 74
  fossils 134, 138, 139
Pterygotus **10**, *10*
Ptilodus 74
Pyrotherium **28**

Q

Quetzalcoatlus **25**, *90*

R

radar 154
radiocarbon dating 133

radioisotopes 132
radiometric dating **132–133**
raptors *43*, *56*, *99*, *99*
rat fossils 139
relative dating 130, 132
reptiles *44*
  early 46
  first 16–17
  fossils 138
  temperature control 20
Rhamphorhynchus 129
rhinoceros 39
  fossil *117*, 139
Rhyniognatha 147
Riojasaurus **51**, *51*
root fossils 119
rubidium-strontium dating 133

S
sabertooth "cat" **37**
  fossils 127
sabertooth "tiger" **36**
Saltasaurus 45
Saltopus 44
Santana Formation, Brazil 138
satellite images 141
saurischian dinosaurs *82*
sauropod dinosaurs **54–55**, *57*, 68, 71
scales fossils 119
scavenger dinosaurs 92, 93
scratch marks fossils 127
sea lions **37**
sea reptiles 22, 24, **62**, 74
sea scorpions **10**
"sea serpent" *135*
seaweeds 8
sedimentary rock 123, 124, 130, 140
seed cone fossil *118*
seed fossils 119, 126
senses,
  dinosaurs **60–61**
shale 124
shark fossils 139
  teeth 120
shell fossils 119
shellfish fossils 138, 139
Shonisaurus 81
Silurian Period *129*
Sinosauropteryx 136, *136*

skin,
  dinosaurs 84, *104*, 149
  reptiles 16
slate 124
Smilodon **36**, *36*
snail fossils 139
snakes 74
Solnhofen, Germany 139, *139*, 153
sperm whale *80*, 81
spiders 14
  fossils 126
Spinosaurus 45, **58**, *58*, **110**
spiny sharks **12**
spores 131
stealing fossils 150–151
Stegoceras 78
Stegosaurus 45, *135*
Steno, Nicolas 120
Stephanoceras 129
stomach stones 55
Struthiomimus 78
"Sue" 95, **106–107**, *106*, 107, 150
Styracosaurus **67**, *67*
Synthetoceras **35**, *35*

T
tails,
  Diplodocus 55
  reptiles 21
  Tyrannosaurus rex 82
tar pit preservation 127
Tarbosaurus **96**, *96*, *98*
teeth,
  dinosaurs **52–53**
  Herrerasaurus 48
teeth fossils 86, *118*, 119
teeth mark fossils 127
temperature control in reptiles 20
tetanuran dinosaurs 82
Tetralophodon **33**
tetrapods 13, 14
therapsid dinosaurs 21, **47**
therizinosaurs **57**
Therizinosaurus *57*, *78*
theropod dinosaurs 89, *99*, *99*
Thylacosmilus **37**, *45*
Titanis **38**
titanosaurs 55
"tongue stones" 120
tortoises 74
trace fossils **127**
trackways *127*

trading fossils 150–151
tree fossils 118, 152
Tremacebus 74
Triassic Period 44, 51, 79, *129*
Triceratops **66**, *66*, *78*, **90**, *90*, 93, *93*
trilobites **10**, *10*, *129*, 131, *131*
Troodon **60–61**, *60*
turtles **62**, 74
  fossils 138, 139
tyrannosaurs (Tyrannosauridae) **98–99**
Tyrannosaurus rex 45, **58**, *58*, *59*, 68, **76–105**, *118*
  cousins **96–101**
  limbs and feet 83, **88–89**
  reconstruction **104–105**, *105*
  senses **84–85**
  teeth 52, *52*, **86–87**, *86–87*, 90, 93

U
Uintatherium **27**, *27*
uranium-lead dating 133

V
Varanosaurus **16**, *16*
Velociraptor 69, *99*, *99*
vertebrates 11
vulture 38

W
warm blood 23
whales,
  early 26
  fossils 118, 139, *139*
  sperm *80*, 81
wolf fossils 127
wombat *139*
woolly mammoth *7*, **32**, *32*, *128*, *133*
woolly rhinoceros 6
worm fossils *119*
worms **10**

XYZ
X-ray 154
Yutyrannus 137, *137*
zone fossils 131

Acknowledgments

The publishers would like to thank the following sources for the use of their photographs:
Key: t = top, b = bottom, l = left, r = right, c = center, bg = background

Front cover illustration Stuart Jackson Carter **Back cover** (tr) Ismael Montero/Fotolia, (c) Michael Rosskothen/Shutterstock, (cr) Catmando/Shutterstock **Endpapers** Roger Harris/Science Photo Library

Alamy 65(t) petpics; 76–77 Photos 12; 96–97 Zachary Frank; 107 David R. Frazier Photolibrary, Inc.; 133(b) sciencephotos, 139(cl) B. O'Kane; 140(b) dpa picture alliance archive; 143(tr) Reuters; 144(br) Felix Choo; 146–147 Peter Phipp/Travelshots.com

Diomedia 136(t) Natural History Museum London UK

FLPA 134(b) Martin B Withers

Fotolia.com 87(tr) DX; 125 Ismael Montero; 130(b) Albo; 131(t) Jaroslaw Grudzinski

Getty 52(br) Layne Kennedy; 86(tl) Corbis/VCG; 102–103(bg), 103(br) & 153(cl) Bettmann; 104(cr) Lynton Gardiner; 113(t) Handout/Getty/IMAX Corporation; 118(bl) Layne Kennedy; 119(bc) Colin Keates; 141(tr) Paul A. Souders/Corbis/VCG; 142–143 Ted Soqui

Glow Images 72(b) O. Louis Mazzatenta; 150 Ladislav Janicek/Corbis

iStockphoto.com 132(bl); 138(c) Saturated

Louie Psihoyos 48(t); 54(cl); 108; 110–111; 145(br); 151(tr); 154(bl)

National Geographic 86–87(c) Jason Edwards

Photoshot 49(b) Picture Alliance

Reuters 69(t) Handout; 106(bl) Handout Old

Rex Features 112(b) Moviestore Collection/Shutterstock; 114–115 Nils Jorgensen; 151(br) Sipa Press

Science Photo Library 42–43 & 57(r) Jose Antonio Peñas; 54–55 Julius T Csotony; 55 Sciepro; 62–63(c) & 74–75 Christian Jegou Publiphoto Diffusion; 65(b) Walter Myers; 69(b) Christian Darkin; 72–73 Steve Munsinger; 105(t) Volker Steger; 116–117 Jim West; 126–127(c) Mauro Fermariello

Shutterstock.com 4–5(t, bg) & 56 Michael Rosskothen; 44–45(bg) Eric Broder Van Dyke; 45(t) & 53(b) Catmando; 46(b) leonello calvetti; 48–49(bg) George Burba; 57(bg) Marilyn Volan; 58(t) Kostyantyn Ivanyshen, (c) Linda Bucklin; 59(bl) DM7, (br) Jean-Michel Girard; 66 leonello calvetti; 67(c) Ozja, (b) Ralf Juergen Kraft; 84(bl) Kanate; 120(bl) Science Photo Library; 137(cr) SmudgeChris; 147(bl) Tinnaporn Sathapornnanont

Topfoto.co.uk 113(b) 2003 Topham Picturepoint

All other photographs are from: DigitalSTOCK, digitalvision, John Foxx, PhotoAlto, PhotoDisc, PhotoEssentials, PhotoPro, Stockbyte

All artworks are from the Miles Kelly Artwork Bank

Every effort has been made to acknowledge the source and copyright holder of each picture. Miles Kelly Publishing apologizes for any unintentional errors or omissions.